W9-DGY-019

CONGREGATIONAL HEALTH

HOW TO MAKE YOUR CONGREGATION A HEALTH-AWARE COMMUNITY

KRISTEN L. MAUK, PH.D.,RN, CRRN-A, APRN, BC
CYNTHIA RUSSELL, DNS, RN
JACK BIRGE, M.D.

HILTON PUBLISHING COMPANY • ROSCOE, ILLINOIS

ISBN 0–9675258–8–8

Copyright © 2003 by Kristen L. Mauk and Cynthia A. Russell

Hilton Publishing Company
PO Box 737, Roscoe, IL 61073
815-885-1070

Notice: The information in this book is true and complete to the best of the authors' and publisher's knowledge. This book is intended only as an information reference and should not replace, countermand, or conflict with the advice given to readers by their physicians. The authors and publisher disclaim all liability in connection with the specific personal use of any and all information provided in this book.

Publisher's Cataloging-in-Publication
(Provided by Quality Books, Inc.)

Mauk, Kristen L
    Congregational Health: How to Make our Congregation a Health-Aware
      Community / Kristen L. Mauk. Cynthia A. Russell, Jack Birge—1st ed.
    p. cm.
    Includes references and index.
    ISBN: 0–9675258–8–8

    1. Health—Religious aspects. 2. Spiritual healing. 3. Pastoral care. I. Russell,
Cynthia A. II Birge, Jack E., 1929. III. Title.

BL65.M4M38 2002   291.1'78321
                                         QBI02–200390

Printed and bound in the United States of America.

To my dear husband, Jim, for your support and love that give me
strength.
To my precious daughter, Rachel, who has always been there for
me with love and affection, in good times and bad.
To my sons, Kenny and Daniel, for bringing me joy.

—KLM

To Richard and Marion Dary, my parents and humble mentors of
a Christ-centered life.
To Douglas Lemster, my loving husband and my strength.
To Blair, Allison, Neil, Joshua, and Stephen, my children and guiding lights.
To my brothers and sisters in Christ at Grand Canyon University,
my fellow pilgrims.

—CAR

To my wife, Barbara Birge, and all the miracles she has brought.

—JB

CONTENTS

PART THREE
COPING WITH HARD TIMES

FOREWORD

For most of human history the individual human body's own defenses were the only protection against disease. In the past, diseases were more likely to be fatal and life spans were short. Today, diseases that once took the lives of thousands are controlled by modern treatments such as antibiotics, immunizations, and specialized surgery. But technology can't replace nature. Despite modern medical breakthroughs, if natural defenses are lost, the success of disease control is also lost.

The body's defenses are numerous and each is important. In the blood, when bacteria enter the body, white cells rapidly increase in number in order to combat them. At the same time, when a person is immunized, or exposed to disease, the body forms chemical substances called antibodies specific to that disease or immunization. These antibodies work to inactivate the invasion.

The human body has still other defense resources in healthy glandular activity and nutritional status. Good diet keeps the immune system healthy and strong and protects a person from illness.

But as important as they are, none of these defenses can do more for the body's health than the core that lies within. This essential force is described in various ways as will to live, inner strength, willpower, good spirit, or determination. Whatever it is called, it can determine the outcome of a disease.

The authors of this book think of this force as spiritual. Spiritual strength may be more apparent in some people than in others, and can rise and fall in everybody, but the essential truth is that spirituality can be strengthened and vitalized.

That's what this book is about: how to understand and assist spirituality in those afflicted with illness, distress, or disease.

That's why we think this book is important: if you help a person know the strength of his or her spiritual nature, you may save that person's life.

I have had the privilege of treating the sick for forty-two years and have had many opportunities to see that maxim at work. I have seen people who were so sick that we doctors gave them little chance of recovery but who beat the odds and got well. I have also seen people not so sick who died because they couldn't find spiritual resources to draw upon.

Strength of spirituality can come from many sources. Some people build it out of their own desire. They realize the importance of the spirit, seek strength from others who are strong, and develop firm convictions, based on religious belief or simply on faith.

Other people need a lot of help to build such strong structures. Often, their spiritual weakness first becomes obvious to them when they suffer severe stress or illness. At that moment, the help of another human being may make all the difference.

There is nothing more important than the force of one human being helping another. I recently read a campaign speech given by U.S. Senator Max Cleland who is a triple amputee–both his legs and one arm were lost from a grenade explosion while he was serving in the military. He recalled the moment when he awakened in the hospital and realized his injuries. A feeling of hopelessness came over him.

Then a nurse came in with a gift. It was a flag sent to him by the men of his military unit. On it were the words "Press on," the unit motto. Suddenly Senator Cleland felt a new strength within, and those words, "press on," continued to provide him strength in his long, arduous struggle to again become a useful human being accomplishing his purpose in life.

Senator Cleland's story teaches us that spirituality, besides helping to cure disease, can assist those who *can't* be cured to obtain the most life can offer.

Religion plays a key role in spirituality, and the vast resources of a congregation can be of great value in building, or repairing, the spirituality of people who are sick and in need. The power of the church can also embrace the families of the sick, who are the burdened support-givers, for they also may need help and encouragement.

I am a scientist and a medical doctor, and I am not qualified to expound on religion. But I do realize its importance. Scientists are especially aware of the orderliness of all that has been created. From my own angle, that couldn't have just happened. It had to come from the power of God.

Religious leaders can have great influence on human spirituality. This book is made to help religious leaders and their congregations become leaders in a campaign for better health in America.

Please consider this book to be a manual for churches, a map that can be used to aid the spirituality of the sick. Who knows? You might save a life.

—Jack Birge, MD

PREFACE

Congregational Health was written as a resource for pastors, deacons, priests, rabbis, lay people, and anyone who works with congregations.

The book is divided into three parts. Part I describes what congregations need to know in order to practice congregational health. It introduces you to the phases of human development, and to health issues pertinent to each phase. Part I also addresses basic spiritual issues—such as how our beliefs and expectations of the world can help shape our emotional and physical well-being, and how we can find and offer comfort.

In addition, Chapter 4 of part I gives a quick-glance reference to the major illnesses you might find among people in your congregation or community, so that you can better understand what a person who is ill may be experiencing.

Part II tells you how:

- to start a congregational health program in your own church.
- to handle emergencies
- to organize activities that help the sick and their families
- to organize activities that make your congregation more aware of its power to help and heal

Part III helps you look at the most difficult issues, such as death or chronic disease, or the emotional anguish of loss. It outlines coping strategies, and also guides you through some of the ethical and legal considerations that are part of dying and death.

This book offers many resources that your congregation may use to promote the health of your faith community and bring comfort to those who are hurting.

Go and serve!

—The authors

ACKNOWLEDGMENTS

The authors thank Dr. Neil Shulman for his help and enthusiasm in developing the idea for this book, and our editor Bert Stern for his suggestions and insights.

My personal thanks must be said to some special people who truly carried me during the valleys of my spiritual life. Thank you to Ma and Pa Bell, who cared for me in the darkest of times, during physical illness and spiritual weakness, and whose unwavering faith brought me hope. And to Marcia Marquardt and Pastor Mike Eddie who, by walking with me through the valley, did not allow me to lose faith in God or His plan for me.

Also, my deepest gratitude to Pastors Steve DeWitt and Don Helton, whose pastoral care and encouragement through the ministries of my home congregation at Bethel Baptist Church in Crown Point, Indiana, helped me on the road to spiritual healing and health.

—KLM

PART ONE
THE ABCs OF CONGREGATIONAL HEALTH

ONE

THE MEANING OF CONGREGATIONAL HEALTH

For centuries, people have speculated about the relationship between health and Faith—that is, between physical health and spiritual health. Prayer has been said to speed healing and decrease recovery time after surgery. Prayer has been linked to miraculous stories of recovery from the brink of death. Prayer can also console people with long-term illnesses, many of whom give witness to the power of prayer to discover and sustain strategies that help cope with serious illness and the physical and spiritual suffering that can go with it .

Many verses in the Bible make a connection between physical health and the emotions, soul, or spirit. *Proverbs* is especially full of wise sayings on the subject:

- "A soft answer turneth away wrath, but grievous words stir up anger." (Proverbs 15:1)
- "A merry heart maketh a cheerful countenance, but by sorrow of the heart the spirit is broken." (Proverbs 15:13)
- " . . . but he that is of a merry heart hath a continual feast." (Proverbs 15:15)
- "Understanding is a wellspring of life to him that hath it. . . ." (Proverbs 16:22)
- "A merry heart doeth good like a medicine, but a broken spirit drieth the bones." (Proverbs 17:22)

As scientists and other professionals continue to explore the connection between physical and spiritual health, health care professionals increasingly believe that they must treat the whole person, not just the body. We have seen cases where indomitable spirit and great faith helped people with devastating illness or injuries return to complete health. We've also seen cases where people simply were engulfed by what seemed like minor health problems.

The still mysterious relationship between health and faith may never be clearly understood, but we accept and believe in its existence because of our clinical evidence.

THE CHURCH AND HEALTH

Historically, the church has been a place for both physical and spiritual healing.

Churches were often sanctuaries for those who were outcast. Sisters in convents cared for the ill and dying. During wars, churches were often converted to hospitals to care for injured soldiers. In virtually every faith, the spiritual being who is called the spiritual leader is believed to have performed miracles, which often involve physical healing.

In the Christian faith, Jesus spent thirty-three years during His earthly ministry performing many miracles, including healing the blind, the lame, the sick, and even raising people from the dead. But while physical healing is the outcome of some of these stories, spiritual healing precedes it, in the form of forgiveness, cleansing, or freedom. As Matthew 9:35 records, "Jesus went about all the cities and villages, teaching in their synagogues, and preaching the gospel of the kingdom, and healing every sickness and every disease among the people."

In the early Christian church, the disciples of Christ continued this tradition of ministering to the sick and diseased. In later years, many Catholic and Protestant nursing orders were formed to care for the sick. Sisters provided nursing care as well as spiritual care. Deacons and deaconesses provided medical services within churches. Nurses worked through parishes, convents, and monasteries and were most influential in the development of our modern-day congregational health programs. Often, such congregational missions have to do with providing care for the poor and sick.

Today, as in earlier times, health promotion and disease prevention that take place in congregational settings are becoming part of the church's work. Let us tell you something about the recent history of the idea of Congregational Health.

FROM PARISH NURSING TO CONGREGATIONAL HEALTH

Nurses have cared for members of their churches for many decades, but the concept was revitalized and modernized by Granger Westberg. Westberg, a pastor, felt that giving health care providers such as nurses a formal position within churches would be an ideal way to combine health and faith ministries, help address the rising costs of health care, and help congregations find their way to the best health resources.

The nurses under Westberg's tutelage became known as "parish nurses," and they used the church or parish, rather than the typical hospital or home-care system, as the setting for their work. Today, the parish nurse movement has spread to all parts of the United States, Canada, Australia, Korea, and many countries in Europe.

According to Phyllis Solari-Twadell (1999), parish nurses promote whole-person health within faith communities. The area of practice is the faith community, and central to practice is the spiritual element.

Solari-Twadell lists seven functions of the parish nurse. The nurse is:

- integrator of faith and health
- health educator
- personal health counselor
- referral agent
- trainer of volunteers
- developer of support groups
- health advocate

From this list of duties, you can see that parish nurses do not follow a medical model of care. Parish nurses are registered professional nurses who go through special training to become parish nurses. They do not perform invasive procedures, nor provide direct care services. Their main emphasis is on education and training rather than on direct physical caregiving.

The teaching they give is based on integrating health and faith and thus meeting the needs of the whole person. Parish nurses teach others how to use the health care system. They provide information about important health issues, and they train volunteers to help in health/faith ministries.

Parish nurses must also be spiritually mature, and they should feel a calling towards this particular type of ministry, with all its special demands. A parish nurse must be able to:

- function independently without the constant presence of other health care professionals that one would find in the hospital setting.
- work as part of a team
- commit to the idea of a healing ministry that is housed and maintained within the local church.

Several programs in the United States offer specialties, a certificate, or coursework in parish nursing.

Parish nurses may work in any one of several arrangements within their churches. They may work part-time or full-time, be paid or act as volunteers. But whatever the arrangement, nurses who work in churches operate under nationally recognized standards to which they are held professionally accountable, as in other specialty areas of nursing.

Many churches cannot afford to pay for the services of a registered nurse (RN). To begin a parish nurse program, money can be raised through grants, donations, or special fund-raising projects coordinated by specific groups within the church.

Parish nurses need networking support. There are often local Parish Nurse Program Coordinators who are hired by a group of churches to manage several sites and personnel. Such coordinators are typically experienced parish nurses who can help the newcomer with orientation, counseling, and continuing education as a program is being started. Regular meetings may be held with local parish nurses to form their own support system and solve problems or discuss pertinent issues.

Special events and speakers may be arranged for the parish nurse network. Newsletters have been used by some groups to communicate information and keep in touch. National conferences are held in large cities, and churches will often raise funds to send their parish nurses to these.

Although parish nursing often leads the way, many churches are beginning programs they call "congregational health ministries" or "congregational health programs." The term "parish" is used most commonly by Catholics, Lutherans, Presbyterians, and Methodists, while the term "congregational" is used by other denominations.

Parish nurses are congregational health promoters, managers, or ministers, and some congregations may give them these titles, or refer to them as health program "coordinators." But although the parish nurse may not be a "minister" in the narrowest sense, the work of coordinating the health/faith program of a church is a kind of ministry. Nurses educated in parish nursing are uniquely qualified to undertake such a position.

DEFINING THE ROLES OF LEADERS

While the nurse serves as coordinator, each member who assists with health care activities within your church will have a clearly defined role. Here are some suggestions regarding those roles.

The *pastor*, generally considered the leader of the church, has ultimate responsibility for making major decisions. But the pastor is usually guided and supported by a group of trusted *elders* or *deacons* who advise him/her and to whom he/she is accountable.

If you as a congregation member want to initiate a congregational health venture, first speak with your pastor to find out whether you should talk to the pastor or to an *assistant* or *associate pastor*, or even a lay leader who oversees special activities. Or perhaps you may be accountable to a newly formed *health committee*. A larger church may already have a *person designated to help with new ministries*.

- In any of these cases, you may need to develop a written proposal to begin a new program.
- It is wise to have one person who is a qualified health professional (such as a registered nurse or physician) to coordinate your program or activity.
- This person should have the heart for health promotion as well as sufficient knowledge and training to make the venture a success.

No matter whom you deal with when introducing congregational health, be sure to define the role of each person who will be involved. Write down names, phone numbers, and addresses of all members of the "team" or "committee" who will help with the particular activity, event, or program, and what their jobs will be. You will thereby avoid much confusion later.

Chapter 5 provides more specific information on starting your own health program.

LEARNING TO WORK WITH THE HEALTH CARE SYSTEM

For people not familiar with how the health care system works, starting a congregational health program may be daunting. Whether you wish to begin with a single, small activity such as free blood pressure screening after church one Sunday, or you are ready to undertake the start of a comprehensive congregational health program, you will have to learn how to work with the health care system.

Today's health care system can look like a tangled web, but if we want to promote health and wellness in our congregations, we must learn to navigate it. *Many congregations employ the services of a registered nurse because nurses are uniquely qualified to help lay people figure out the system.* They are trained to find and utilize community resources and to educate others about how to keep healthy and prevent disease.

Let us use the example of Terry Smith. Terry is a registered nurse who felt called to educate the senior citizens in her church on how to stay healthy. Several older adults in her large congregation had suffered strokes that past year, and the pastor wondered if, with education, some of these strokes could have been prevented. He asked Terry for suggestions.

After some thought, Terry recommended doing monthly blood pressure screening with the help of the local hospital where she worked. She also recommended that the congregation schedule a talk by a hospital staff member about reducing risk factors for stroke. She suggested that this talk take place at the next church meeting of the seniors' group.

Her pastor liked Terry's ideas and referred her to the director of ministries on his staff. The director worked with Terry to get regular blood pressure screenings approved by the deacon board. Terry knew how to use the hospital's standard forms in determining referrals for abnormal blood pressures. The hospital's educational staff not only arranged for monthly screenings but also donated free pamphlets to her large congregation. In addition, they provided a qualified speaker for her educational program.

For the program to work, Terry had to develop resources *within* the congregation as well. She enlisted nurses in the congregation to volunteer to help take blood pressures on a rotating basis. Several people with dangerously high blood pressure were identified and referred to the hospital for further tests. Two of them required treatment from their family physicians. The educational program on reducing risk factors for stroke also worked well. People asked questions of the speaker, and several of the older adults made lifestyle changes.

While Terry's program focused on a single health issue—the dangers of high blood pressure—the activities she planned became the basis for a comprehensive congregational health program.

Terry's story suggests some tips about working with the health care system:

- Find someone who has a connection to the local hospital and get to know them.
- Use nurses in your congregation as resources.
- Identify the appropriate places to refer people to with their health needs.
- Have a plan for dealing with medical emergencies that might occur at the church itself. (See chapter 6.)

Now you have the basics. Later in this practical guide, you will find still other suggestions for promoting health within your congregation. We encourage you to think about what you can do within your own faith community.

REFERENCE

Solari-Twadell, Phyllis Ann and McDermott, Mary Ann: *Parish Nursing: Promoting Whole Person Health within Faith Communities.* Thousand Oaks, CA: Sage Press, 1999.

TWO

HEALTH FROM BIRTH TO OLD AGE

You enter the sanctuary as the service begins and your eyes
scan the congregation. As you look to the left, you notice
Jenny and Mike, a young couple filled with expectation as
they await the birth of their first child. Just ahead of them, John sits
with his head bowed in prayerful reflection. You remember the
many years that Sarah joined him in that very pew. They had been
married nearly fifty years when Sarah died of lung cancer last year.

Suddenly, your eyes dart in the opposite direction as a shriek of
joy explodes from two-year-old Tina as her five-year-old brother
makes a silly face. Their adolescent sister, Lorna, is mortified, while
their parents exchange knowing glances. As the service starts, you
whisper a word of blessing on these and all members of the congregation, thankful for the richness of your work.

As an elder of your congregation, someone to whom others turn
for wisdom and leadership, or as a minister or priest or rabbi, or as
any congregational member who understands why good health care
is so basic a human right, you know that *in order to promote good
health within the congregation, you must first understand basic
human development.*

This chapter explores some of the major developmental milestones from conception to late adulthood, providing a snapshot of
the physical, cognitive, and psychosocial development that occurs at

each of life's stages. As always, we especially focus on topics of particular relevance to health ministry within the church.

THE PRENATAL STAGE TO BIRTH

Conception occurs when a sperm and an ovum (egg) combine to form a zygote. The one-celled zygote divides, becoming an embryo (two to eight weeks) and then a fetus (two months to birth).

All of the biological information required for development of the human body is present at conception. In other words, the body knows all it needs to know to carry out its miraculously complex tasks.

During the next thirty-eight weeks, growth and development of the unborn baby occurs at an amazing rate. The mother's nutritional state, age, drug intake, health status, physical activity, and exposure to environmental hazards affect the prenatal environment of the fetus. It is significant that most birth defects and miscarriages occur in the first three months of the pregnancy. Up to twenty percent of all pregnancies end as a miscarriage, often without the woman's knowledge.

Labor occurs in three stages. During the first stage, the cervix dilates to about four inches. This stage lasts about twelve to twenty-four hours. Contractions are often painful, usually increasing in frequency and duration as labor progresses through this stage.

The second stage, lasting about one and one-half hours, begins when the baby's head moves through the cervix, and ends with the baby's full emergence.

The third stage entails the delivery of the placenta, or afterbirth.

In the United States, most deliveries occur in the hospital, often with the father present. For low-risk pregnancies, birthing centers or home birthing may be an option. Childbirthing classes may reduce the need for medication during the birthing process and support the parent's comfort level with the delivery.

In the United States, approximately twenty percent of the babies born are delivered by cesarean section. Cesarean delivery is the surgical removal of the baby from the uterus. The cesarean is a significant surgical procedure that can increase the recovery time for the birth experience.

Though most babies are born healthy, some are born too soon or are too small. A preterm (premature) infant is born before the completion of thirty-seven weeks' gestation. A low-birthweight infant weighs less than five and one-half pounds at birth, while very low-birth-weight babies weigh less than three and one-third pounds. Advances in the medical care of these high-risk babies has improved survival rates and reduced serious consequences of preterm birth.

Many factors contribute to the birth of underweight infants. Some identified risks include:

- being a mother under the age of seventeen or over age forty
- living in poverty
- being African-American
- being single
- having a low level of education
- having inadequate or no prenatal care
- smoking
- having poor nutritional habits
- using drugs or alcohol
- having multiple pregnancies
- having certain health conditions

Efforts to reduce or eliminate these risk factors, where appropriate, can help decrease the number of low-birthweight babies.

Pregnancy
Pregnancy is a time of transition, whether it is a long-awaited event or comes as an unintended surprise. You can help in this transition by promoting opportunities for the pregnant woman or couple to discuss their hopes and fears associated with the pregnancy, birth, and child. If the pregnancy is not welcomed, then the woman or couple may seek you out for religious counsel and guidance.

Infertility
Infertility, the inability to conceive a child despite trying for one year, often results in feelings of pain, frustration, and isolation, espe-

cially from God. Problems with conception are divided fairly equally between men and women.

A thorough medical evaluation may help the couple determine the cause of the condition. The medical team will offer recommendations for promoting conception. New advances in assisted reproductive technologies (ART), including in vitro fertilization (IVF), are available. IVF combines sperm and eggs in a laboratory for a baby that is genetically related to one or both partners.

The couple may look to you for guidance from church doctrine for issues of implantation of multiple embryos, the use of donor eggs, and disposition of frozen embryos. In addition to moral aspects of this issue, ART is expensive and there are no guarantees of success. Infertility can put great stress on the couple, so your support is extremely important.

Loss of the Pregnancy

Loss of the pregnancy through miscarriage, stillbirth, or death of the newborn is an emotionally devastating experience that will require your support. The parents attach feelings to the unborn child, whether this child is desired or not. Grief is a natural reaction, and parents can feel isolated when the larger community does not recognize the extent of their loss. You can play an important role in supporting the parents through the grieving process and helping them adjust to their loss. You can do this by offering spiritual guidance and promoting compassion in the congregational community.

Stressful Pregnancy

Certain pregnancies, such as those involving multiple births, can be very stressful for the couple. Twins, triplets, and other multiple births can be difficult to carry to term. Multiple babies are often born preterm and with low birth weight. The numbers of multiple births continues to rise because of the use of fertility drugs and ART. In this area, the congregation can provide spiritual and practical support for the couple, so that they can face the challenges of high-risk births.

Birth Defects

When the infant is born with a birth defect or other serious health condition, the parents are certain to feel threatened by the situation. Not only are they exhausted by the birthing experience, they are faced with the less than perfect child of their dreams and all of the complications related to the infant's care.

In addition to helping them through the grief process and providing spiritual comfort, you may be able to assist them in better navigating through the confusing medical environment that is thrust upon them.

Postpartum Depression

Many people think that the days following the baby's birth are—or should be—extremely happy for the new parents. This can be true, but even the most well-adjusted parent may sometimes feel down during this period.

A new mother, in particular, has to respond to rapid changes in her body, including hormone levels, physical exhaustion, and unaccustomed demands. For most women, this emotional disruption is short-lived. However, about ten percent of women who have given birth experience a condition known as "postpartum depression" (sometimes, "postpartum blues").

Although postpartum blues for most women does not mean deep or lasting depression, we have all read or seen tragic stories in the media about mothers of newborns or young children acting on urges to hurt themselves and/or their children. Be attentive to postpartum blues; help the mother get professional help when that is required.

Older Siblings

If older siblings exist in the family with a newborn, remember to pay special attention to them. It is easy for them to feel left out when their new brother or sister is receiving so much attention. Make it your special mission to seek them out, to let them know that they are special children of God, and that they too are loved.

INFANCY AND TODDLERHOOD
(BIRTH TO AGE THREE)

The time from birth to three years of age is an explosive period of growth and development. The average baby is twenty inches long and weighs seven and one-half pounds at birth. By five months, the infant doubles his/her weight and grows about one inch per month through the first year. The birth weight typically triples by the first birthday, with steady and rapid growth continuing, though slowing by the third year.

The typical newborn will sleep sixteen to seventeen hours a day and will consume about fifty calories per pound of weight per day.

The newborn has some basic reflexes, called "primitive" reflexes, which are evident at birth and disappear within the first year of life:

• The *sucking reflex* occurs when something is placed in the mouth, allowing the infant to receive nourishment.
• When the baby's cheek is stroked with a finger or nipple, the baby will turn its head, open its mouth and begin sucking. This is known as the *rooting reflex*.
• The *moro reflex*, or *startle response*, occurs in response to a sudden, loud noise or the sense of being dropped. The newborn extends its extremities, arches its back, and draws back its head.
• When an infant grasps something placed in its palms, the baby is demonstrating the *grasping reflex*.

These and other reflexes give way to a rapid progression of gross and fine motor skills over the next months and years. Most babies are able to grasp a rattle at age four months and can roll over by five months. At seven months, many babies are able to sit without support and can stand with support by nine months. Grasping with the thumb and finger develops at about this time as well for most infants.

The skill of walking well happens for ninety percent of all children before the age of fifteen months. As the child becomes mobile, he/she will continue to refine and enhance gross and fine motor skills. By twenty-four months, most children will begin to run and jump in place, and can kick and throw a ball. Most children will be toilet trained by the age of three.

Cognitive skills progress rapidly from birth to three years of age.

Gradually, the infant learns to coordinate information gathered from his/her senses. Memory develops and the infant will repeat actions and become increasingly involved in his/her environment.

Actions become more deliberate and purposeful. Basic problem-solving skills are evolving as the baby approaches his/her first birthday and continue to develop at a rapid rate.

Language development really involves physical, cognitive, emotional, and social components. Newborn crying progresses to cooing, laughter, and playful sound patterning in a matter of months. By nine months the baby understands some words and by around one year of age the baby says her first word. At two years, most children have a vocabulary of at least 400 words and begin putting them together to form short, two word sentences.

Psychosocial development for the infant involves emotions, temperament, and experiences with others, especially the parents. Though the emotions of distress and interest are present at birth, other emotions develop over time, progressing from anger, joy, fear, sadness, shyness to jealousy, shame, guilt, and pride.

Temperament relates to the infant's unique personality, behavioral style, and how he/she approaches life. Many children are easy-going, generally happy, and easily adapt to new situations. Some have temperaments described as difficult—that is, they are harder to please, irritable, and expressive of their emotions. Another group of children tends to warm to changes around them slowly. Many children are a unique blending of all of the temperaments described above.

The process of becoming part of a family is a major developmental component of the life of the young child. Attachment, in infancy, is the bond between the caregiver(s) and the infant.

Noted psychologist Erik Erikson identifies the period during infancy and up to eighteen months as the time when the infant deals with developing basic trust versus basic mistrust. At this time, the infant develops a sense of the world as a good and safe place (trust).

But mistrust can occur when the baby determines that the world is not a safe place.

Between ages one and three, the child moves on to Erikson's second stage, called "autonomy versus shame and doubt." In this stage the child begins to do things independently of his/her parents—things such as walking, climbing, deciding what to eat, and exploring. Success with these accomplishments pushes the child to become even more independent. Parents who are overly critical or overprotective may cause the child to feel doubt or shame.

Congregational Support for Parents of Infants and Toddlers
If your congregation has many young families, consider offering parenting classes and parenting support groups. Most parents welcome opportunities to compare notes and share stories about their adventures and misadventures in parenting. Often parents realize that others are experiencing many of the same frustrations and questions that they are, along with the joy and fulfillment of raising a family. Your classes should include the basic milestones for the infant's physical, cognitive, and social development. As the "incredible (versus terrible) two's" approach, you can offer suggestions to create a positive and supportive environment for the child and his/her parents. Do not forget to talk about the importance of safety in the home and car. Also, encourage these young families to stay up-to-date on their well-baby checkups and immunization schedules. Be sure to provide opportunities for single parent families to participate in the classes. Consider providing childcare services during the parenting classes.

The use of day care services is of particular concern to most young families. Since more than half of all mothers (and nearly all fathers) with children under the age of one work, childcare is an important issue. Some families are choosing to have one parent stay in the home, forgoing a second income. For many families, especially single parents, this is not a viable option. You can provide a valuable service to your congregation by discussing the qualities of a good day care arrangement. Many churches actually provide childcare services. Does your church offer the best day care services possible? If not, what can you do to improve them?

EARLY CHILDHOOD
(AGES THREE TO SIX)

Physical growth continues at a quick pace, though it is slower than in infancy. Children at this age are able to engage in many activities because of the progress made in motor development. Boys and girls are able to run, skip, jump, hop, and throw balls in early childhood. They can draw pictures with crayons or markers, button their shirts, and tie their shoes, all demonstrations of the advancement of fine motor skills.

The advances made in cognitive development continue at a rapid rate. During early childhood, children use symbols, meaning they think about something without needing it in front of them. The ability to organize or classify objects begins during these years. Children understand numbers and learn to count. The many "why" questions asked by three to six year olds are evidence of developing cause and effect thinking. Parents and others need to remember, however, that the thinking of the young child is still evolving and still not logical.

In early childhood, language skills continue to progress with an increase in vocabulary and more application of grammar and syntax. Parents with questions about delays in their child's language development should discuss their concerns with their health care provider.

According to Erikson, resolving the tension between initiative and guilt is the task of early childhood. Initiative refers to the child's efforts to engage in purposeful activities, while guilt can occur as a result of experiencing disapproval from others for these activities. Play, and especially imaginative play, is an important way for children to develop social and cognitive skills. At this age, boys tend to be more aggressive than girls. Children learn about gender roles by modeling the behaviors of the culture and start to align themselves with friends of the same sex. The self-concept, or how one views one's own self, begins to evolve.

Congregational Support for Parents of Young Children
Congregations can provide support for parents of young children by offering parenting classes. Reminders about child safety issues are especially effective in preventing accidents. Other important topics to discuss might include:

- sleep disturbances
- bed-wetting
- discipline

Health Promotion Programs for Young Children
It is never too early to teach self-care and self-love as a reflection of God's love. Young children enjoy learning about their bodies and discovering how to stay healthy. You could do a "glow germ" program on hand washing, in which the children can actually see how germs can remain on the hands if thorough washing has not occurred. Food is always popular with this age group, so maybe a simple nutrition class serving fun fruits and vegetables would be a hit.

The options are limitless, so use your imagination.

MIDDLE AND LATE CHILDHOOD
(AGES SIX TO TWELVE)

As you take notice of the school-age children of your congregation, you are probably struck by the variety of shapes and sizes. Six to twelve is a broad range of ages, but we can make some general observations:

These children grow about one to three inches each year and gain five to eight pounds.

Early on, the boys will tend to be taller and heavier than the girls, but around age ten, girls experience a growth spurt.

Motor Development in Middle and Late Childhood
In the middle and late childhood years, motor development becomes more coordinated and children are faster and stronger than they were before. Mastery of physical skills becomes important to children, and both girls and boys engage in organized sports.

Sports programs can offer wonderful opportunities for children to learn to compete, develop team-building skills, enhance self-esteem, and work out regularly. However, increased competition and pressure from parents and coaches can cause children to experience stress in relation to their sports activities. The pressure to achieve can be excessive, and should be managed carefully.

Mental Development in Middle and Late Childhood
In middle and late childhood, children develop the ability to solve concrete problems. They can think logically because they can consider multiple factors at once. Children in this age group begin to take on more of a world view, and are able to see other peoples' points of view. Their ability to work with numbers and to recognize individual things in relation to their classes (that is, to see that this object belongs, for example, to the class, "chair") continues to develop. Memory, language skills, and communication improve significantly during middle and late childhood.

Moral Development in Middle and Late Childhood
According to developmental psychologist Jean Piaget, moral development advances in middle childhood. Piaget considers younger children guided by fixed and rigid rules. Children see behavior as either right or wrong and believe that punishment is the consequence of misbehavior. Older children are able to incorporate other peoples' viewpoints and understand that right and wrong are not absolute. In this way, they develop their own moral code that is characterized by flexibility.

Obesity
In the United States, many children are already obese by the middle childhood years. A child (or any other person) is considered obese if he or she is more than twenty pounds over what medical experts consider his or her "ideal" weight. *Too little time spent in exercise, too much in passive activities like viewing television, and the consumption of processed, high calorie foods are at least partially responsible for the increased numbers of obese children.*

School

School becomes a central focus in the early and middle childhood years, affecting every aspect of children's physical, cognitive, emotional, and social development. Children with special learning needs such as those with mental retardation, attention deficit hyperactivity disorder, and learning disabilities will require special attention.

Erikson suggests that the task of middle childhood is "industry versus inferiority." The child develops a sense of competence when he/she is able to master skills and finish tasks. If a child struggles in this area, he/she is at risk for feeling inferior to peers and others.

Family Roles and Relationships

Parents continue to play the most important role in the lives of children during middle to late childhood. Family roles, relationships, and responsibilities are very significant in children's development. Remember that many nontraditional family structures exist in the United States.

Some authorities suggest that alternative family constellations, such as same sex couples, may create additional stress for children, though many same-sex couples learn to minimize such stress.

Children of divorced parents may live with one parent or both and may have half-siblings or step-siblings. Lower school achievement and other social problems are associated with children living with one parent or in step-families.

Congregational Support for Parents

Maintain support through parenting classes with special attention to concerns about child safety, especially now that the children are older and more mobile. Children are naturally adventuresome and think little about danger until it may be too late. Discussions with parents and their children about the dangers posed by strangers are appropriate at this time. Facilitating discussions on positive approaches to discipline could be especially helpful for parents.

A health promotion program for children in this age group should focus *on the children's sense of self in order to promote their sense of self-worth.*

Adolescence
(Ages Thirteen to Eighteen)

Adolescence is the transitional stage between childhood and adulthood. A period of physical change, adolescence may also involve cognitive, emotional, and social upheaval.

Adolescence starts with the onset of puberty, or the beginning of sexual maturity and the ability to reproduce. For many Americans, adolescence begins well before the age of thirteen, and perhaps as early as age seven; adolescence may continue for some young people into their early twenties. Many young people postpone the responsibilities of adulthood until educational or training programs are completed.

Rapid growth in weight and height occurs with the onset of puberty, along with muscular and skeletal development. Girls and boys will reach nearly their full height by age eighteen.

Along with sexual maturity, body proportions and form change. Females produce increased amounts of estrogen leading to the development of breasts and the growth of female genitals. The first menstruation, or menarche, begins the process of shedding tissue from the lining of the uterus each month. The increase of testosterone in males stimulates body hair and growth of the male genitals. The production of sperm is the primary sign of sexual maturity in males.

Adolescents in your congregation will mature at different rates. In a group of thirteen and fourteen year olds, some teens will have been sexually mature for two or three years, while others won't develop sexual maturity until two to three years later.

Adjusting to early maturation or late maturation can present a special challenge for young people. Studies indicate that early-maturing boys tend to adjust more easily than early-maturing girls.

While an adolescent goes through important physical changes, he or she is going through mental ones as well. Adolescents develop the ability to think abstractly, using hypothetical-deductive reasoning. Teens are able to sort through a variety of theories and options, work through false answers, and arrive at conclusions that they consider to be true.

Closely related to these new cognitive abilities is moral development. As early as age thirteen, according to theorist Lawrence Kohlberg, some people can make judgments related to basic principles of fairness, justice, and what is right.

The basic question for adolescents, according to Erickson, is "Who am I?" Young people work toward understanding themselves in terms of occupation, values that they will live by, and sexual identity. This long-term process involves experimentation and exploration. Many young people continue to work on issues of identity into their twenties or beyond.

Sexual orientation is a significant component of a teen's developing identity. Is the young person sexually interested in members of the opposite sex (heterosexual) or in those people of the same sex (homosexual)? Secular controversy continues as to whether sexual orientation is determined before birth or afterwards. If a teenager experiences feelings that conflict with his or her religious beliefs, this time can be extremely confusing and difficult. Therefore, providing an open and trusting environment in which teens are given the opportunity to discuss their feelings is critical in this process of acknowledging their sexual orientation.

Many teenagers become sexually active—putting themselves at risk for sexually transmitted diseases, pregnancy, and emotional trauma. Open discussions about sexuality in the home and church are important in guiding young people to make the best decisions regarding their physical, emotional, and spiritual well-being.

Congregational Support for Adolescents and their Parents

A *health promotion program* focusing on the special concerns of adolescence can be invaluable for both adolescents and their parents. Holding concurrent but separate classes for teenagers and parents allows each group to be more comfortable by first sharing their experiences, concerns, and fears with their peers. Kinds of subjects that might come up include:

• the use of drugs and alcohol
• high-risk behaviors
• juvenile delinquency

- sexual activity
- pregnancy
- suicide
- eating disorders

Such classes create the possibility of continued discussion and problem-solving at home. They also strengthen the ability of children and parents to express shared concerns and love for each other.

Community experts can be invited to speak to discussion groups. The credibility of the speaker is especially important to teenagers. Sometimes, teens or adults who have personally experienced any of these situations can also address the groups, and will enjoy the attention and respect of their peers.

Be prepared to assist parents (and teens) in finding qualified health professionals in the community to help sons or daughters who are already experiencing drug or alcohol abuse, sexual issues, legal trouble, or mental health concerns. (In part two you will find more information about where you can find the professional help you need.)

EARLY ADULTHOOD
(TWENTIES THROUGH THIRTIES)

Young adults, their growth complete, are considered the healthiest age group in the United States. Peak physical performance occurs in young adulthood, with an emphasis on endurance and strength. This very physical vitality sometimes leads young adults to believe that they are indestructible. Death by accident is second only to death from AIDS in this age group. In early adulthood, people are likely to develop good or bad habits that affect their health, such as how much and what they eat, whether or not they are overweight, whether or not they exercise, whether or not they smoke and drink.

Teenagers learn how to think, can see more than one point of view, and are also developing strong intuitive approaches to knowing. The process of sharpening the logical faculty continues in adulthood. Adults are more flexible and freer in their thinking.

These changes go along with more obvious changes. Young adults finish their education and move out of the parents' home to seek their first position in their chosen field. Young adults expect downsizing and changes in the employment scene to define their work lives and may change positions many times over the course of their careers, often moving between quite different fields. If they have poor skills, they may also have to experience the stress of working at low-paying jobs.

In a broad sense, we have been describing the route by which people find out who they are. It is a route rich in opportunities, hurdles, and hazards. According to Erickson, the young adult makes the choice between intimacy and isolation. Intimacy means the ability to commit to a close, personal relationship. Love and having children, as Erikson sees it, are evidence of successful completion of this stage. Those who are unable or afraid to commit to a relationship will be isolated and self-absorbed.

Congregational Support for Young Adults

Young adults face many demands in establishing their careers, relationships, and families. Health programming at the church should relate to issues that hold the greatest significance for them. For example, parents of young children may feel they cannot afford to miss a session on child safety in the home. Launching a specific series of programs about relationships and understanding the self may be a way that the congregational health program can benefit young adults.

MIDDLE ADULTHOOD
(AGES FORTY THROUGH SIXTY-FIVE)

The middle years include a host of physical changes that announce, "You aren't as young as you used to be." Some of these changes are associated with aging, while others relate to lifestyle decisions. In middle adulthood, skin wrinkles, teeth yellow, hair turns gray and/or falls out, and a few pounds of weight may be added. Alterations in the senses become evident in middle adulthood, especially changes in sight and hearing. Most people age forty and older require reading glasses to help them see close objects and printed text.

By the fifties or sixties, the reduced blood supply to the eyes leads to a diminished visual field and increased blind spot.

Sensitivity to high pitches is usually the first decline noticed in hearing. Taste and smell also decline in middle adulthood, leading many people to complain that food seems blander than it did years ago.

Another sign of aging is a reduction in height when spinal disks compress. Muscle strength is reduced in the middle years, though consistent exercise can increase muscle bulk. Coordination and reaction time is diminished with aging, though experience and knowledge can compensate for these changes.

Women
The ability to reproduce ends in middle adulthood. Menopause, when a woman's menstruation stops and she can no longer conceive a child, usually occurs between the ages of forty-five and fifty-five, with an average age of fifty-two. At this time, the ovaries and adrenal gland produce progressively less estrogen.

This decrease in estrogen production may result in nausea, fatigue, insomnia, "hot flashes," and vaginal dryness, and other symptoms. Emotional changes such as anxiety, depression, and irritability do not occur as a consequence of menopause, though for years these changes were attributed to the "change of life." Though some women report a decrease in sexual desire, others report no change.

If the symptoms are severe or the woman has concerns about heart disease, osteoporosis, or Alzheimer's disease, she may decide to take estrogen replacement therapy (ERT). Women at risk for breast cancer may decide not to use ERT, since some studies suggest that estrogen may increase their risk for developing cancer.

Men
Though men do not experience the equivalent of menopause, the levels of testosterone do decrease over time, leaving them less fertile than in their younger years. Most men maintain their ability to father a child as they age. About five percent of men at age forty experience erectile dysfunction, or impotence. That is, they are unable to achieve or maintain an erection for a satisfying sexual experience.

Many health conditions, use of alcohol or drugs, smoking, and anxiety may contribute to impotence. Men may wish to discuss this concern with their health care provider because several treatment options, such as medications, surgery, or therapy may reverse this condition.

For most men and women, the middle years continue to be relatively healthy. Fewer than ten percent have serious health problems, which include:

- Diabetes
- Depression
- Anxiety
- Arthritis
- Heart disease
- Hypertension
- Cancer

Cognitive Abilities in the Middle Years

Cognitive abilities remain relatively stable in the middle adult years. Recent memory may decline, especially if serious health conditions exist. For example, the middle adult may have difficulty remembering an address that he or she used the day before. Some suggest that adults continue to improve problem-solving skills and more effectively use intuitive skills over the years. They are better able to deal with complex issues at work and in their personal lives. This is another way of saying, "Wisdom comes with age."

According to Erikson, the middle adult confronts the task of working out the conflict between *generativity* and stagnation. "Generativity" refers to the guidance the middle adult can offer to the next generation through parenting, teaching, and mentoring. Stagnation occurs when the adult is inactive and focuses only on self-interests; then, life may begin to feel very small.

New Family Roles and Relationships

For many middle adults, this is a time of transition within the family. Often children are leaving home ("the empty nest"). Recent research has questioned the long-held belief that this time is difficult for parents, especially mothers. Parents who have not prepared for this transition may be challenged by having time on their hands, but most parents welcome the increased freedom and ability to be creative.

It sometimes happens, of course, that adult children, because they are experiencing marital, employment, or financial troubles, come back home to live with their parents for brief periods or even permanently. While these returns can mean big adjustments on both sides, they can also mean joy, especially if grandchildren are involved.

Middle-aged adults often help to provide support or care for their aging parents, which is why this group is sometimes called the "sandwich generation," because people are caring for their own children as well as their parents. There is obviously stress and strain associated with these responsibilities, but many adults speak of the satisfaction they feel in being able to give back to their parents and thereby develop a deeper relationship with them.

Congregational Support for Middle-Aged Adults
Health promotion programs are particularly well received by middle-aged adults. They know their bodies are changing and that they are aging. This makes them especially ready to take part in discussions on diet and nutrition, exercise, managing menopause, weight management, and stress management.

We recommend classes that focus on specific health concerns during middle adulthood as well. Many people might attend a series on heart health and related conditions such as:

- Hypertension
- Stroke
- Coronary heart disease

  Other topics could include:

- Mental Health
- Cancer
- Osteoporosis
- Diabetes

Finally we recommend that you organize a support group to provide counsel and assistance to the caregivers in your congregation.

LATE ADULTHOOD
(AGE SIXTY-FIVE+)

More than 34.5 million, or one in eight, Americans are over the age of sixty-five, and these figures are expected to rise. *The exciting news is that not only are people living longer, but they are also healthier.* But living longer and healthier lives means understanding one's health. Your congregational health program can help late adults learn how to take better care of themselves and can encourage them in the good work they're already doing. You can begin by understanding the changes that occur with aging.

Physical Changes Associated with Aging
Though the brain does lose mass over a lifetime, dendrite growth actually increases through the seventies. Dendrites are the part of nerve cells in the brain that help to carry messages. What it boils down to is that older adults have the equipment to maintain intelligence and the ability to learn.

Older adults do experience a slowing in their ability to process information. They may also experience deteriorating senses of sight and hearing. Day and night vision, even with the assistance of glasses, may be weakened. Cataracts, cloudy areas in the lenses of the eyes, cause blurred vision in over half of people over age sixty-five. (Surgical removal of cataracts is usually very successful.)

By age eighty-five, nearly half of the population experiences hearing loss that affects daily living. Hearing aids can help, but many older adults find the accompanying magnification of background noises so annoying that they do not wear the aids. A reduction in the ability to smell and taste is also common for older adults.

Strength, coordination, and reaction time are reduced with aging, though this can vary from person to person. The best way to limit a decline in these areas is regular exercise. For example, weight training can lead to increased muscle strength even for people over age the age of ninety. Stretching exercises are of great benefit to the elderly, as is walking, even if walking must be assisted.

Sexual activity continues in later life, though usually with less frequency than in previous years.

Late adulthood can mean the beginning of chronic conditions—diseases characterized by a slow onset and long duration. The most common disease is arthritis, followed by hypertension, hearing impairment, and heart conditions.

The most common causes of death in the elderly are heart disease, cancer, and stroke.

Reaching Clarity and Wisdom

Though changes do occur in our thinking processes as we age, older people continue to learn and to use what they know. Many will complain of weakened memory. But people vary significantly in which mental skills they keep, which they lose, and which they strengthen. Good physical health in late adulthood seems to go along with good mental health.

The key issue of this stage of life, as Erikson sees it, is *integrity versus despair*. At this stage, the older adult reviews his or her life. A person who is satisfied with his or her life achieves what Erikson calls "integrity," or wholeness. Conversely, a person who can find no meaning in his or her life will experience despair.

Robert Peck, a follower of Erikson, suggests that adults need to redefine their worth beyond their work. After a lifetime of valuing the self in terms of its productivity, the older adult must learn to value the self at some deeper level. At the same time, older adults must find a way to transcend the physical body and come to terms with their own mortality.

Adults who are healthy, financially secure, have a social life that involves family and friends, and are active usually have the best adjustment to retirement. For many, the role of grandparent or great-grandparent is a very fulfilling component of their lives.

Older adults continue to live in the community, often with their spouse or other family members. Sixty percent of people eighty-five years and older actually live alone. It may be surprising that only four percent of people age sixty-five and older live in nursing homes. Most people prefer to live independently in late adulthood, but it is important to assess the quality and condition of each person's living situation individually.

Congregational Support for Older Adults

In late adulthood, people benefit from healthy *eating and regular exercise*, to keep themselves healthy and to recover from illness. Your congregation may wish to launch health promotion activities that promote healthy eating and exercise. Such a program can educate both old and young about the special concerns of aging, and can help your older members feel better and live longer.

Because it is sometimes difficult for older adults to come to church for programs, *consider providing home visits to check in on homebound seniors and help preserve their sense of connection with the community.* You might also need to mobilize volunteers to help older adults get to their health care providers or to help them pick up medications. *Do not forget the special needs of your members who are hospitalized or living in institutions.*

Financial concerns may put constraints on the quality and quantity of health care received by older people. *Most seniors qualify for some medical benefits, though they may need you to help them secure these* benefits.

Older adults need to cope with multiple losses including physical changes, retirement, and the deaths of loved ones. Provide opportunities for people to talk about their losses and offer your comfort and instill hope through spiritual support.

THREE

CULTURE AND HEALTH

Marilyn Laszlo, a Bible translator who spent over twenty-five years among a tribe in Papua, New Guinea, tells how, when she was a young missionary, she viewed what appeared to be a funeral in the community where she had been sent. She recounts her horror in seeing the tribesmen burying a young boy who was unconscious but still breathing. Marilyn told the witch doctor conducting the death ritual that the boy was not dead yet—they could not bury him alive! But the witch doctor told her harshly, "White woman, be quiet! You do not know anything!"

This was Marilyn's introduction to learning that death in the Sepik Iwam culture was defined as being unable to move or speak on one's own, not by signs that she had been taught, such as the prolonged absence of breathing and heartbeat.

Just like Marilyn, we may be strangers to a culture that is foreign to us. True, most of us will not have to feel the extreme conflict that Marilyn did in dealing with such a heart-rending situation. But we still need to observe, listen, and learn. *In order to minister effectively to other people, we need to understand ourselves first*, then learn about them and how we are both similar and different.

People's health is often influenced by the practices of the culture of origin, or the culture in which the person lives. In order to promote health within our communities and congregations, we all need to understand what is meant by "culture" and how it affects the way we live.

The many components of culture will be discussed in this chapter. We will also provide you with strategies for becoming more culturally sensitive, both as individuals and as faith communities.

WHAT IS CULTURE?

There are many different ways to define "culture." A simple definition would be that *culture* means those attitudes, feelings, values, and beliefs that influence the way people act and how they live. There are numerous components within a culture that help define it, including race, gender, age, sexual orientation, religion or spirituality, living arrangements, finances, education, employment, and uniqueness. When we are trying to understand a culture different from our own, we must consider each of these factors. This chapter outlines those strong forces that make up a culture and gives you clear suggestions about how your new knowledge can help your congregation and community achieve better health and happier lives.

RACE AND ETHNICITY

Many people think of culture as a person's racial background. Race is certainly part of culture, but it is only one aspect. The word *race* refers to one group of people whose identify is based on physical appearance. The term *ethnicity* encompasses race and includes language, dress, history, and the sense of being part of a unique group.

There are several major ethnic or cultural groups within the United States including Anglo- or European-American, African-American, Hispanic/Latino, Asian-American, and Native American. Each of these groups will be discussed later in this chapter.

GENDER

Many health problems are associated more with one gender than another (see Chapter 4). For example, osteoporosis is more prevalent among females, while spinal cord injuries are more often found among males. In addition, women are more likely to be providers of health care than are men and women have a longer life span than men—the statistical list goes on.

Considering gender issues can help you plan a more relevant and useful congregational health program. If your group is largely female, think about the group's unique health care needs.

Perhaps you would include more educational programs on subjects that uniquely affect women, such as menopause, female health problems, incontinence, pregnancy, and delivery. If a group is predominantly male, consider programs that target stress reduction, prevention of cardiovascular disease, or prostate cancer screening.

AGE

Many churches have attendees that range in age from newborns to the very old. Other churches have a larger percentage of older adults. The particular situation of each congregation would definitely influence the types of ministries in which the church may want to invest. Older adults experience more chronic illnesses, and usually more hospitalizations and health complications.

Children are prone toward accidents. A child-rearing family has very different needs from the older couple whose children are grown and moved away. And adolescents face their own particular hazards.

As you work to devise a plan that addresses the health concerns of each age group in your church:

- Think about the concerns of each group and how age influences each situation.
- Find out which age groups have the greatest needs in your church group and begin there.
- Consider bringing in a speaker from a local medical or nursing school to talk about the aging process and how to combat the effects of old age.

SEXUAL ORIENTATION

This sensitive area is hard for most churches to deal with, but the nature of today's American society makes it necessary for us to be increasingly aware of the differences among us—including issues of sexual orientation. Church members can be sensitive to differences in sexual orientation without condoning certain practices. The ability to accept another person's choices when they are in conflict with your own does not mean you promote those actions. Too often differences in sexual orientation, such as being gay, lesbian, or transgender, are the source of estrangement and stigma within families and churches. Because it is not a subject much discussed in the church community setting, families in the midst of this struggle feel isolated and often ostracized.

For example, a single mother, call her Ann, has just been told by her twenty-year old son Jason that he is gay and plans to marry another man. Ann raised her son in the church as a single parent. Now she feels that she has failed to convey the truths most important to her. She blames herself for Jason's lack of a father figure but she cannot accept the lifestyle he has chosen.

Ann's pain goes even deeper than that. She can't turn to the people she'd ordinarily turn to for help. She is unable to share her thoughts and grief with the people in her church because she is embarrassed and ashamed, and she does not wish to tell other family members for the same reason. Ann is also afraid that Jason will contract HIV because of his sexual practices. So she decides to cut off all contact with him until he "comes to his senses."

Imagine the loneliness and confusion of both mother and son in this sad situation. Then think about how your congregation might reach out to people in similar situations. Here are some suggestions for getting started:

- Have your pastor or other spiritual leader introduce the subject in a sensitive way.
- Invite a noted speaker on this sensitive subject to a special educational meeting.

- Try not to be judgmental: listen to the person who is hurting.
- Educate your congregation about HIV and AIDS to dispel myths.

RELIGION AND SPIRITUALITY

A distinction between the terms *religion* and *spirituality* may be helpful here. Religion refers to organized worship or faith, like what takes place in the denomination you belong to, such as Catholic, Baptist, Buddhist, Muslim, or Jewish. Spirituality is more general, referring to one's own feeling of being connected with a higher power. Thus, a person could consider him or herself spiritual without being religious.

Religion and spirituality are key components of most cultures. Religious practices and traditions provide continuity, help define our lives, and provide help and comfort in times of crisis. For Christians, baptism cleanses the recipient of original sin and marks the person's entry into the faith community. Bar Mitzvah and Bas Mitzvah play a somewhat similar role among Jews. And for many faiths, marriages are often performed in the church setting and taken to be a sacred covenant.

There are many other examples of how a person's spiritual beliefs are closely linked to particular practices. Catholics believe it is essential that a priest anoint a sick person prior to the time of death. Most Buddhists are cremated. Hindus and Buddhists believe in reincarnation. The use of alcohol is forbidden in Islam. Jehovah's Witnesses are excommunicated if they receive a blood transfusion. Orthodox Jews will eat only kosher foods.

We must keep that influence in mind, even when we are ministering to people in our own congregations. We have to know what people think and feel about their own situations, and what they hope and fear, before we can be of much help to them.

FINANCES, EDUCATION, AND EMPLOYMENT

Finances, education, and employment have closely related influences on culture and may also help determine a person's health status. For example, as a person becomes better educated, he or she may be able to get a better-paying job and more insurance benefits, thus positively influencing his or her health and that of the family. Conversely, if a man lacks education and takes a job working in a factory from which he is then laid off, or a woman lacks education and ends up working in a fast food restaurant with low wages and few benefits, their finances will suffer.

People in lower socioeconomic groups often have poorer access to medical facilities and health care than other groups. The uninsured or underinsured often suffer from illnesses and diseases that are left untreated because they lack funds to pay for needed health services.

Insurance is costly, and there are probably people within your community and even your congregation without health insurance. They do not have to be older people or even out of work. Some teenagers make only enough to support themselves but do not receive health benefits from their place of work. A struggling single parent who puts herself through school and works part-time does not have health benefits for her children. A man who lost his job could no longer afford to pay the out-of-pocket expenses for medical coverage for his pregnant wife. Each of these situations can thrust a family into a lifetime of trying to pay back medical expenses from a catastrophic illness or accident.

Education and socioeconomic status are closely related and one often influences the other. Better-educated people are usually in a higher socioeconomic group. But education need not be the privilege of the few. Your church can be a place of education about health practices and disease prevention. You can teach people how to reduce risk factors, how to get help when they need it, how to take medicine regularly. As an added benefit, your congregation may find that, as gifts and grants come in to assist these efforts, it becomes financially stronger.

Employment is another factor in the cultural equation that

becomes especially important in times of economic trouble. People often derive a sense of satisfaction and even a sense of identity from their jobs. If that job is lost, personal uncertainty can lead to depression and poor health.

Fortunately, funding for clinics in underserved areas has increased at both state and national levels. Often termed clinics for the "working poor," these sites provide basic health care services for people who cannot afford more traditional health plans. Your congregation can help people whose finances keep them from getting the health care they need.

Here are some questions churches can ask to help people in the community who do not have medical coverage:

- What are your community resources?
- Is there a free clinic in your area?
- What services do they provide and for whom?
- Could the person you are trying to help qualify for Medcaid (a state-run health program for the poor and disabled)?
- Are there people in your community who could help someone find a job
- What skills does the person have that could be useful?
- Could there be a job within the faith community for that person?

Here are other ways congregations can help:

- Develop links and connections with those agencies in your community that provide the necessary help. Keep in mind that there may be programs already in place but not well-advertised.
- Invite a speaker from a helping facility to be a guest at your next women's luncheon.

Living Arrangements

The place that we call home helps define who we are. People within one community often have similar housing and even similar living arrangements. We all know when we're in a rich neighborhood or a poor one. And even where people may live in straw huts, those huts are the living style of that community.

In America, the way our home is arranged helps tell others what we value and who we are. Our homes often reflect our personal tastes and desires, the things we treasure. The phrase "keeping up with the Joneses" is frequently used in a lighthearted attempt to minimize the need to conform and even achieve a higher standard of living.

But the most striking example of how living arrangements influence culture is that of the homeless. Homelessness is a widespread problem in most major cities. You may even be able to think of someone you have seen in your own town who walks about the streets during the day pushing a shopping cart or carrying multiple bags or rummaging through the trash.

The homeless are typically stigmatized by society and they have little access to health care. For them, health care may seem like a luxury, since they also lack food, shelter, clothing, transportation. They may live in cardboard boxes, in alleys, or under bridges. They may sleep in homeless shelters or even on a bench in the train station or airport. In certain cities, the homeless population is so great that city workers pass out cardboard boxes each evening for people to sleep in. Other cities confine their homeless to specific neighborhoods to "hide" them from more upper-class areas.

Many people who become homeless have physical, emotional, and psychological problems. But others were working professionals who fell on bad times and were unable to recover because they lacked sufficient resources and help.

So what can you do? Here are some suggestions:

- Find out if there are homeless people living in your community and how widespread the problem is.
- Talk to local social service agencies about what is being done to address the homeless problem.
- Become familiar with all of your community resources.
  Work with your local agencies and government to offer help.
- Make regular donations to food pantries, or set one up in your own church.

- Come up with still other ways that your church can be of direct help to the homeless.

PERSONAL UNIQUENESS

People are unique and some people have obvious differences that may cause them to be left out within a group setting. It may be a physical deformity such as a birth defect, or a disability such as cerebral palsy, or even having to use some adaptive equipment such as a wheelchair or walker. Anything that makes a person different from the cultural norm can cause them to feel apart from the group.

Additionally, some professionals believe that those with certain illnesses or diseases form their own type of cultural groups based on the processes they must go through in the course of their lives.

RECOGNIZING YOUR OWN CULTURAL HERITAGE

The first step in becoming more sensitive to the cultures of others is to be familiar with your own. This task should be purposefully undertaken in order to develop cultural sensitivity to others. Consider some of the following questions about your own cultural heritage:

- What are some of your family traditions? How long have you practiced them? How much do you value your traditions?
- Where did your grandparents live? What is their country of origin? What generation are you? (For example, you are first generation American if your parents migrated from another country but you were born here.)
- What religious practices are important to you? What religious dates do you observe?
- Are there special holidays or celebrations unique to your family?
- How important is extended family?
- What is your standard of living?
- What is your general health status? How much do you value the health care system?

• Do you have unique practices in the area of health? (For example: dietary restrictions or use of certain folk medicines.)

A tremendous richness can be obtained by appreciating and sharing cultural differences. People will find that exploring other cultures and other faiths helps them clarify and appreciate their own in addition to providing a wealth of knowledge about others.

Most people believe their own culture is the best, but that attitude may often spring from prejudices such as racism, ageism, and sexism. By knowing yourself and the significance of your own culture, you may be better prepared to recognize and respect those who come from very different cultures.

Start this human task by evaluating your own cultural sensitivity. Ask yourself these questions:

• Do I accept others who are different from me?
• If a person who is "different" comes to visit my church, do I go up and introduce myself?
• How do I feel when I see a homeless person?
• Do I harbor any negative feelings, thoughts or attitudes toward people of other races, the elderly, adolescents, or the other gender?
• Would I be willing to serve in a soup kitchen during the holidays?
• Is there anything that I am doing now to help those less fortunate than myself? What else could I be doing?
• How do my children react to people who are different? To those with a physical deformity? To those who are poor? To those who live in a run-down neighborhood?
• Do I try to keep up with the next door neighbors? Do I feel I have to have the newest car or the biggest house on the block?
• Do I believe that being sensitive to people who are different from me is part of the mission of my church? Part of my personal mission? Something I should be doing to demonstrate my faith?

AMERICAN CULTURES AND HEALTH

We stated at the beginning of this chapter that it was important to try to gain some knowledge about cultures different from our own in order to understand how culture influences health practices. Now we want to describe the five major ethnic groups within the United States. In order to describe them we must generalize, but the reader must realize that each culture has a set of subcultures, and each subculture can be unique. *The reader is advised not to stereotype*, but to use this basic information as a springboard for inquiring into the culture of people within their community and church.

Each person is unique and none should be forced into a predetermined mold based on race or ethnic background. The intent of this section is simply to provide some basic facts about each of the five major groups (Anglo-Americans, African-Americans, Hispanics/Latinos, Asian-Americans, and Native Americans), and to give some examples of how culture influences their health practices.

Anglo- or European Americans

These are the terms used for those who are Caucasian, white, non-Hispanic individuals. Overall, Anglo-Americans have higher educational levels, better incomes, better health, and longer lives than most other groups. There are many subcultures within this group, such as those who are Jewish, Italian, French, Irish, German, or Polish. Each of these subgroups has unique traits that make them distinct. Traditions are plentiful and ties to the country of origin tend to be passed down through generations. Anglo-Americans typically value beauty, wealth, success, and health. They are generally family oriented.

African-Americans

African-Americans have a significant history that helps to define their culture. With their roots in slavery, African-Americans have suffered many years of discrimination and cruelty in the United States. Though this situation has improved, discrimination and cruelty still goes on.

African-Americans are at a disadvantage in many health areas. They have the highest poverty rate of any of the major minority groups. Older African-Americans tend to be less healthy, have more chronic illnesses, and have less access to health care. Younger people are often at higher risk than their Anglo counterparts. Their life span is significantly less than that of Anglo-Americans.

One significant problem among African-Americans is hypertension, or high blood pressure. Over half of the people in this group are affected, often at a younger age than people in other population groups. This can lead to heart disease and stroke.

While African-Americans may lack the community resources that others have, they typically have strong social support through the family. Religious upbringing and strong church affiliation are also an integral part of life for many African-Americans, as is a strong belief in life after death. The primary religions found in this group are Protestant (with a large number of Baptists) and Muslim. A strong religious heritage is often passed down through generations.

In the African-American culture far more than in Anglo-American culture, the elderly are respected and their opinions valued. Intergenerational living arrangements are common. Strong family ties often mean that the disabled and elderly are cared for at home. Home remedies for illnesses are common, and may be tried before traditional health care. While presumably there is at least as high a percentage of depressed African-Americans as Anglos, African-Americans are reluctant to report depression.

Finally, if people have had a negative experience with the health care system, they likely will mistrust health care professionals. Many African-Americans know how, at Tuskegee Institute, medical experiments were performed on African-American subjects that were not in their best interests. Such memories die hard.

Hispanics/Latinos

There are many different subgroups of Hispanics, though the majority of the Hispanic population in the United States is of Mexican origin. In this varied culture, there are strong family ties within a structure where the men are usually dominant. Extended family is very important and there is a deep sense of loyalty and commitment and respect to the family. Older adults are held in high regard.

Spanish is the primary language spoken, and elderly Hispanics may not speak English, making communication in some instances difficult. The major religion is Roman Catholicism. Respect is a key factor in this culture, so people may be reluctant to complain if they think they are imposing on another person.

Prayer, rosaries, medallions, candles, and folk remedies are commonly used. The folk practitioner, called the *curandera,* uses healing powers, herbal remedies, and rituals to care for persons in his/her culture. Health and illness may be viewed as either rewards or punishments from God. There is a strong belief in the afterlife.

Asian-Americans

The Asian-American group includes the Chinese, Koreans, Vietnamese, Japanese, and many others. This group is most like Anglo-Americans in terms of financial status and stability. People generally experience good health.

Family ties are also strong among these subgroups, with the family unit being the dominant structure. Elders are revered. Being a single person in this culture may result in isolation. Eye contact may be avoided because it may signify disrespect.

Although Asian-Americans typically use traditional Western medicine, they also frequently practice folk medicine and home remedies. Many alternative modalities used now in the Western world originated in the Chinese and Japanese culture. These include techniques such as acupuncture, herbal tonics, and acupressure.

Chinese and Japanese cultures often think that illness is caused by an imbalance in the life force called "chi," and refer to positive and negative forces that represent good and evil, hot and cold. When chi is disrupted, the body is out of balance. The body needs to be in a state of harmony to maintain health. A calm and peaceful environment is valued.

Confucianism, Taoism, and Buddhism are common religions.

Native Americans

There are many different tribes among Native Americans, each with unique belief systems and cultural practices. Use of tribal artifacts during religious ceremonies is common. Their religious practices often involve worship of spirits related to nature, animals, and Mother Earth.

Native Americans are among the most deprived cultures in America. Many live in poverty. Similar to African-Americans, Native Americans were also a repressed and enslaved people. Displaced from their homes, about one fourth of them still live on reservations. There is a widespread problem with alcoholism and diabetes in this population. Many Native Americans lack access to the health care system and are more inclined to use folk cures.

Personal space should be maintained when speaking with a Native American person. As a sign of respect, avoid direct eye contact. Native Americans may not speak openly of their health problems or their religion.

Increasing Cultural Sensitivity in the Congregation

People can feel frustrated and helpless when dealing with people from cultures different from their own—so much so that a mother can even get estranged from her son. People have trouble accepting other cultural practices because these practices may conflict with their own beliefs about what is right and wrong, what is valued and what is not.

The best way to remedy our blindness toward, or prejudice against, other cultures is to observe and listen to people who are different from ourselves and examine personal feelings about our own cultural roots. Then we can begin to appreciate others. *Members of the congregation should try to learn all that they can about differing cultural beliefs and practices* so that when differences arise, as they are apt to within groups with a high mix of cultures, they will take advantage of a great opportunity to educate one another. Make sure this sensitizing process is undertaken in a non-threatening, non-judgmental manner.

Here are some suggestions for getting started:

- Keep the main goal of your health program at the forefront of discussion and do not allow individual agendas to detract from that goal.
- Develop your own cultural sensitivity and encourage congregational members to be open and hospitable to people different from themselves.
- Devise ways to deal with conflicts that arise.
- Make a plan to include different cultural traditions in your church activities or programs.

F O U R

UNDERSTANDING
COMMON ILLNESSES

Diseases and medical terminology can be hard to understand. By learning the ABCs of the common health problems people in our faith communities face daily, and by
understanding what they are going through physically, emotionally,
and spiritually, we can learn to provide comfort and healing. At the
same time, we can learn to be better custodians of our own and our
family's health.

This chapter does not contain a complete list of illnesses. We
chose to present some of the more common medical problems seen
in typical congregations and give you basic general knowledge as
well as suggestions or strategies to help people who are suffering or
on the road to healing.

We think it's important for any health-aware community to
understand all the basic medical information we offer here. While
your congregational team is studying all this information, pastors,
deacons, youth workers, and other volunteers will find it useful to
look up particular diseases or conditions as they encounter them
among their members.

If you need to know more about a medical problem, turn to the
resource list for that problem. Most of the listed organizations provide free information and may also alert you to other related health
issues.

HOW TO USE THIS CHAPTER

In this chapter, we have tried to keep things simple. The chapter is divided into eight sections according to areas or functions of the body. The ninth section addresses emotional, psychological, and spiritual concerns. Here are the sections:

- Heart, lungs, and circulatory problems
- Brain, spinal cord, muscle and nerve disorders
- Gastrointestinal and internal organ problems (stomach, intestines, bowels, and other internal organs)
- Reproductive, sexual, and urinary conditions
- Skin and bone problems
- Ear, nose, and throat problems
- Blood and hormonal disorders
- Other medical conditions
- Emotional, psychological, and spiritual concerns

Each section follows a specific format to allow the reader to get the basics of each medical problem at a glance. The terms used are listed here:

Description: A brief explanation or summary of the problem

Incidence: How common or rare is the problem? (More information and statistics may be given in parentheses.)

Prevalence: Is this condition more common in males or females, young or old, one ethnic background or another?

Sign and Symptoms: A list of common signs or complaints that might be found or experienced if a person has this problem

Risk factors: A list of circumstances that would increase a person's chances of having this problem; many of these circumstances are controllable, but some are not; minimizing risk factors as much as possible prevents certain diseases

Usual treatment: Most common ways of treating the problem

Recovery Time: A general idea of whether the problem is short- or long-term, and whether it is curable or incurable

Spiritual Considerations: Tips on particular things to think about or do when offering spiritual support

Suggested Scriptures: A verse or verses from the Bible that might be particularly helpful or meaningful to the person with this problem; most are general, but some are more specific to the particular illness or suffering that the person may be experiencing; the reader should evaluate each suggested reference for its appropriateness to each person's unique situation

Resources: Places to write or call for further information; websites that appear particularly helpful; lists of major organizations dealing with particular disorders

Though we present current information about each problem listed, no book can replace the care or advice of your physician or primary health care provider. This book is a tool to help you familiarize yourself with some of the problems your friends and neighbors may have, and to provide a few suggestions about how you can help.

We caution you against diagnosing your own or other people's problems. Many health problems have similar signs and symptoms, and only a qualified medical professional can make final judgments as to diagnosis and proper treatment.

Heart, Lungs, and Circulatory Problems
Angina
Description: Lack of oxygen to the heart muscle due to narrowing of the arteries to the heart muscle, reducing blood flow and oxygen supply, causing chest pain. When blood flow is restored, or demand for oxygen by the heart muscle is reduced by rest, the pain goes

away. This condition differs from a heart attack in that no death of heart muscle occurs.

Incidence: Common (can occur in any individual with diseased coronary arteries)

Prevalence: Males more than females; most common in middle-aged and older men; also seen in postmenopausal women

Signs and symptoms:
- Shortness of breath upon exertion
- Chest discomfort or heaviness (may radiate to neck or arms)
- Weakness
- Cold sweat

Risk factors:
- Family history of coronary artery disease at a younger age
- High blood pressure
- High cholesterol
- Smoking
- Diabetes
- Advanced age
- Male gender

Usual treatment:
- Medications (to dilate coronary arteries –nitroglycerine under tongue)
- Lifestyle changes (stop smoking, minimize stress, low fat/low cholesterol diet)
- Sometimes surgery is indicated

Usual course: Occurs episodically, usually lasting about fifteen minutes and never longer than thirty minutes. Pain lasting longer than thirty minutes must be considered a heart attack. More frequent episodes of angina can herald the worsening of coronary artery disease and indicates the angina may be unstable.

Spiritual considerations: If pain or shortness of breath occurs during an activity, have the person stop and rest. Find out if he or she has known angina and whether or not he or she takes nitroglycerin. Most people with angina carry nitroglycerine with them in a small, dark bottle. If symptoms are not relieved by three doses each taken five minutes apart, then take the person for emergency treatment.

As with any heart problem, this disorder can be frightening. Keep the person calm and provide comfort.

Suggested scriptures: Psalms 27:14; Psalms 29:11

Resources:
American Heart Association
7272 Greenville Avenue
Dallas, TX 75231
214–373–6300
www.americanheart.org

Asthma
Description: A disorder in which airflow is obstructed in the small airways of the lung from spasm of the muscles in the lung walls, causing them to become smaller in caliber and limit the passage of air. Wheezing is characteristic of this disorder, because air can get in better than it can get out. Asthma is thought to be an inflammatory response that may be triggered by allergies (to molds, dust, animal dander, feather pillows), smoke, infections, exercise, or stress.

Incidence: Common (ten million new cases per year; seven to nineteen percent of those cases are in children)

Prevalence: More common in children and young adults, but may occur at any age; males more than females until puberty, then about equal; if onset is in adult years, females more common than males

Signs and symptoms:
- Wheezing
- Cough
- Increased heart rate
- Struggling to breathe
- Attacks and remissions

Risk factors:
- Family history
- Viral respiratory infections in infancy

Usual treatment:
- Medications (to reduce inflammation and open the airways—often including inhalers for regular use)
- Eliminate the sources that trigger reactions

Usual course: Asthma is usually a lifelong illness. The incidence and severity of the attacks vary. When attacks are severe, seek medical attention as soon as possible.

Spiritual considerations:
- Flare-ups can be a medical emergency.
- Have a plan for your congregation to follow in the case of asthma attacks, which can be life-threatening in some people.
- During an episode, remain with the person and help him or her stay calm.

Suggested scriptures: Isaiah 12: 2; Acts 17: 24–28

Resources:
Asthma and Allergy Foundation of America, Suite 305
Washington, DC 20036
1–800–7ASTHMA
http://www.aafa.org/

Atherosclerosis (commonly called Hardening of the Arteries)
Description: A form of cholesterol invades the walls of the arteries due to excessive amounts of it in the blood. It damages the blood vessel walls as it builds up, forming *plaques* that look like flaking paint. Continued buildup can eventually impair blood flow at narrowed places in the arteries, even to the point of total obstruction of some of the vessels.

Incidence: Common

Prevalence: Males more than females until menopause, then about equal

Signs and symptoms: Usually no observable symptoms until a vessel is narrowed or blocked by a clot, then symptoms vary depending on where the vessel is blocked (i.e., brain = signs of stroke; heart = signs of myocardial infarction)

Risk factors:
- Hypertension
- Smoking
- Diabetes
- Obesity
- Advanced age
- Family history
- Sedentary lifestyle
- High fat diet
- High cholesterol
- Male gender

Usual treatment:
- Lifestyle changes (low fat diet and other dietary controls; increase physical fitness; stop smoking; restrict alcohol intake)
- Medications to lower cholesterol

Usual course: Avoiding risk factors and taking medications, along with exercise, can greatly reduce chance of death related to this disorder

Spiritual considerations:
- This is a long-term problem for many people, especially older men. Take time to listen to their concerns.
- Encourage compliance with the treatment plan.
- Consider starting an exercise group or have a dietician come to talk with your Seniors in order to emphasize prevention. Take a proactive approach.

Suggested scriptures: Isaiah 40:31; Psalms 103:5

Resources:
American Heart Association
7272 Greenville Avenue
Dallas, TX 75231
214–373–6300
www.americanheart.org

Bronchitis
Description: Inflammation of the airways and lungs due to an infection; can be acute or chronic

Incidence: Common; more common in smokers and those with allergies that have large amounts of lung mucus

Prevalence: Males equally with females; all age groups; chronic type is more common among the elderly

Signs and symptoms:
- Cough (with sputum)
- Fever
- Aching

- Fatigue
- Chest congestion

Risk factors:
- Chronic lung disease
- Very young and very old
- Smoking
- Alcoholism
- Allergies
- Air pollution
- Sinus infections

Usual treatment:
- Rest
- Drink plenty of fluids until fever is gone
- Medications (antibiotics are given when the sputum is yellow)
- Lifestyle changes (stop smoking; restrict alcohol; control risk factors)
- Evaluation for allergies

Usual course: In acute type, good prognosis with proper treatment; in chronic type, can be serious and recurring

Spiritual considerations:
- If acute, provide care and comfort. Give reassurance that treatment will ease the symptoms and speed recovery.
- If chronic, strengthen social and spiritual support systems.

Suggested scriptures: Isaiah 41:10; Psalms 57:1

Resources:
American Lung Association
1740 Broadway
New York, NY 100019
(212) 315–8700
www.lungusa.org

Congestive Heart Failure (CHF)

Description: CHF is the main complication of heart disease in which the heart cannot pump well enough to meet the body's demands. This occurs when there is weakening of the heart muscle, decreasing the heart's output. This results in blood backing up in the lungs—thus the term congestive heart failure. CHF can occur as the result of any type of heart disease, such as heart attack, leaky valve, inflammation of the muscle, and others.

Incidence: Common (one of the most common inpatient diagnoses for older adults)

Prevalence: Males more than females before age seventy-five, then about equal

Signs and symptoms:
- Trouble breathing
- Lung congestion
- Wheezing
- Fast breathing
- Fatigue
- Ankle swelling
- Weakness

Risk factors:
- Heart problems
- Not taking medications as prescribed
- Excessive stress

Usual treatment:
- Medications (to reduce blood flow to heart and increase output of heart)
- Lifestyle changes (controlling risk factors; identifying causes; fluid and salt management in diet)

Usual course: Follows the course of the heart disease causing it. As the disease progresses, episodes of congestive heart failure increase to the point of becoming intractable and leading to death

Spiritual considerations:
- As with any heart problems, people may express fear and anxiety; provide comfort.
- If the person is hospitalized, visit regularly, as the situation may change from day to day.

Suggested scriptures: Psalms 25: 14–22; Psalms 73: 26; John 14:27

Resources:
American Heart Association
7272 Greenville Avenue
Dallas, TX 75231
214–373–6300
www.americanheart.org

Cystic Fibrosis

Description: A progressive, chronic, and eventually fatal lung disease caused by a recessive genetic defect that causes mucus in the lungs to be very thick, leading to recurrent infections and lung destruction.

Incidence: Most common deadly genetic disease (one in 2000 births among Anglo-Americans)

Prevalence: Mainly diagnosed in infants, children, and young adults; males more than females; seen less in African-Americans, Asians, and Native Americans than Anglo-Americans

Signs and symptoms:
- Wheezing
- Chronic cough
- Cyanosis

- Barrel chest
- Failure to thrive
- Clubbing of fingers
- Pale skin
- Recurrent respiratory infections
- Struggling to breathe

Risk factors: Family history

Usual treatment:
- Medications
- Care by an experienced interdisciplinary team
- Respiratory therapy
- Oxygen when needed
- Regular exercise
- Healthy diet high in protein and calories

Usual course: Chronic and progressive; there is no cure. Treatment is aimed at thinning the lung secretions and preventing and treating infection. Death most often occurs in childhood, though patients are living longer because of the newer, more potent antibiotics.

Spiritual considerations:
- A most difficult diagnosis for children and families to hear—offer continual support.
- Be aware that parents may lose more than one child to cystic fibrosis since it is genetic in nature.
- The end result of this disease is a difficult death related to respiratory failure or complications preceded by months or years of medical treatment; strengthen social and spiritual support network; develop a long-term plan.
- Help patients and families feel less isolated by making regular home visits if church attendance is not possible.
- Educate youth in the congregation about the disease and encourage them to give support to the child who suffers from this disease and "feels different" from everyone else.

Suggested scriptures: Psalms 34:18; Psalms 40: 16–17

Resources:
Cystic Fibrosis Foundation
6931 Arlington Road, Suite 2000
Bethesda, MD 20814
1–800–344–4823

Heart Attack (also called Myocardial Infarction {MI})
Description: Impaired circulation to the heart muscle due to blockage of one or more of the arteries that supplies the heart muscle. When this occurs, blood cannot get to the area supplied by this artery, and the heart muscle dies.

Incidence: Not uncommon (600 per 100,000 in the US)

Prevalence: Males more than females until age seventy, then equal

Signs and symptoms:
- Crushing chest pain
- Pain that radiates to the jaw or shoulder
- Squeezing, heavy feeling in the chest
- Complaint of bad indigestion (especially seen in the elderly)
- Sweating
- Pale skin
- Nausea, vomiting
- Dizziness

Risk factors:
- High cholesterol
- Sedentary lifestyle
- Stress
- Heredity
- Obesity
- Smoking
- High blood pressure

- Advanced age
- Angry personality
- Diabetes

Usual treatment:
- Medications (to lower cholesterol, control high blood pressure, dilate arteries to the heart, prevent and dissolve clots, reduce the heart workload)
- Angioplasty and/or surgery if indicated
- Lifestyle changes
- Cardiac rehabilitation

Usual course: The event occurs suddenly with sudden death (cardiac arrest) in about twenty-five percent of cases. With procedures to restore circulation to the heart (bypasses or angioplasty), recovery is rapid, usually within two weeks. However, months of cardiac rehabilitation are recommended.

Spiritual considerations:
- Denial of the condition is common during a heart attack.
- Physical presence and good listening skills may help allay common fears.
- If heart surgery is indicated, fear of death is often present.

Suggested scriptures: Psalms 27:13–14; Psalms 43:5

Resources:
American Heart Association
7272 Greenville Avenue
Dallas, TX 75231
214–373–6300
www.americanheart.org

Hypertension (high blood pressure)
Description: Sustained blood pressure above "normal." American Heart Association defines high blood pressure as "greater than or

equal to 140 mm Hg systolic pressure or greater than or equal to 90 mm Hg diastolic pressure." (www.americanheart.org)

Incidence: Common (about fifty million Americans; twenty percent of the US population)

Prevalence: Males more than females; more common among African-Americans

Signs and symptoms: Sometimes called "the silent killer" because there are usually no symptoms until it becomes a significant problem; sometimes headache is reported. The absence of symptoms means that the only way you know you have it is to have your blood pressure taken. Diagnosis is made by several episodes of elevated blood pressure and is not based on a single measurement (since blood pressure can fluctuate from a variety of factors).

Risk factors:
- Obesity
- Family history
- High salt diet
- Stress
- Alcohol
- Sedentary lifestyle

Usual treatment:
- Medication
- Dietary restrictions
- Lifestyle changes (weight loss, smoking cessation, exercise, relaxation)

Usual course: Often chronic. High blood pressure is not curable. It is, however, controllable. If allowed to progress uncontrolled, it may lead to a crisis which may be of sudden onset (such as heart attack, stroke, or kidney failure). Any of these events may lead to rapid death.

Spiritual considerations:
- Instill hope.
- Encourage compliance with treatment to reduce risk of stroke.
- Use of prayer and meditation to help reduce stress levels.
- Recognize that medications taken for hypertension may cause sexual dysfunction.

Suggested scriptures: Psalms 55:22; Philippians 4:4–7

Resources:
American Heart Association
7272 Greenville Avenue
Dallas, TX 75231
214–373–6300
www.americanheart.org

Pneumonia

Description: An infection of the lungs that can be caused by several different types of germs, including both bacteria and viruses.

Incidence: Common; bacterial type (800 to 1,200 per 100,000 people in the U.S. each year) most pneumonia in children is viral

Prevalence:
- Males more than females
- Children and older adults more often than the ages in the middle range
- A common cause of death in the elderly

Signs and symptoms:
- Cough
- Fever
- Chest pain
- Chills
- Dark, thick sputum
- Lung congestion

Risk factors:
- Very old or very young age
- People with impaired immune systems (such as AIDS)
- Diabetes
- Heart and lung disease
- Malnutrition
- Smoking
- Alcoholism
- Kidney failure

Usual treatment:
- Medications (antibiotics)
- Respiratory therapy
- Rest
- Proper diet

Usual course: Acute; with treatment, symptoms should improve within days. Some germs are much more difficult to eradicate and have the capabilities of rapidly leading to death. Recovery from pneumonia caused by these types of germs can take weeks and in some cases months.

Spiritual considerations:
- As with any respiratory disorder, difficulty breathing may cause fear and anxiety; provide comfort and a quiet environment for the person to rest.
- Promote hope with the realization that treatment usually helps the person to feel better within days and that this is a short-term illness.

Suggested scriptures: Isaiah 26: 3–4; Philippians 4:19

Resources:
American Lung Association
1740 Broadway
New York, NY 10019

(212) 315–8700
www.lungusa.org

Tuberculosis (TB)

Description: A disease caused by a bacterium notoriously difficult to eradicate. It usually infects the lungs, but it can involve any of the body's organs. It is most often transmitted through airborne particles from a person with active TB.

Incidence: Varies; 9 to 32 per 100,000 people in the US. This was a much more common disease in the past. It then became rare with the advent of antibiotics, but now has become more common, occurring frequently in nursing home residents.

Prevalence: Males more than females; any age

Signs and symptoms:
- Cough
- Fever
- Night sweats
- Weight loss

Risk factors:
- People with a compromised immune system
- People exposed to someone with active TB (especially in airplanes, due to the recirculation of air)
- The following groups:
  - Homeless
  - Migrant workers
  - Health care workers
  - Institutionalized (nursing homes, prisons, mental facilities)
  - Foreign-born

Usual treatment: Medications (now in tablet form; sometimes given by injection). No simple medication effectively eradicates the germ (bacillus). A three-drug program is now being used with considerable success. Confinement in a TB hospital is no longer necessary.

Usual course: Recovery is usually complete given time and compliance with treatment

Spiritual considerations:
- TB is on the rise in many communities. Encourage congregation members to have a yearly TB test. The health department often provides these tests for little or no charge.
- Treatment may take months but generally has a good prognosis. Encourage the person with TB to stick with the prescribed medical plan and give hope that the treatment will help.
- Provide tissues throughout your facility to help prevent the spread of respiratory infections.
- Those congregational members with coughs (for any reason) should refrain from working in the nursery until they are well.

Suggested scriptures: Psalms 103: 2–5

Resources: www.tuberculosis.net

Varicose Veins

Description: Enlargement of superficial veins in the legs that result from problems with valves in the veins. A normal leg vein has a trapdoor-like valve about every three inches that prevents backflow of blood in the vein when the individual is erect. If these valves become incompetent, pressure in the veins increases and the vein becomes larger.

Incidence: Common (about twenty percent of American adults)

Prevalence: Most common among middle-aged females with family history of varicose veins; also common in people who are obese; also more common in women after pregnancy

Signs and symptoms:
- Curvy, bulging, large veins in the legs
- Leg cramps or aching
- Fatigue
- Swelling of the legs

Risk factors:
- Lots of standing
- Wearing restrictive clothing
- Pregnancy

Usual treatment:
- Rest periods with legs elevated
- Light elastic stockings
- Avoid restrictive clothing
- Medications injected at the site
- Surgery

Usual course: Chronic and persistent throughout a lifetime. Uncontrolled, the condition can lead to permanent enlargement of the legs and leg ulcers. The most effective method of treatment is use of adequate support hose (stockings must fit tightly). In many cases, compliance is poor and the disease progresses.

Spiritual considerations:
- This disorder can affect the person's self-image because of the obvious physical changes in the legs. Promote a positive self-image by emphasizing the person's strengths.
- In older adults, wearing support hose and resting often with the legs elevated is preferred to surgery or vein stripping. Thus, the person may have to learn to live with this problem. Offer continued emotional support.

Suggested scriptures: 1 Samuel 16:7; Isaiah 26:3– 4

Resources: http://www.buedu/cohis/cardvasc/vessel/vein/varicose.htm

BRAIN, SPINAL CORD, MUSCLE, AND NERVE DISORDERS

Alzheimer's Disease (AD)

Description: A progressive and degenerative disease of the brain (of unknown cause) that results in increasing mental deterioration that begins with memory loss but leads to a demented state and complete disorientation.

Incidence: Common (forty percent of those over age eighty-five)

Prevalence: Females slightly more than males; age over sixty)

Signs and symptoms:
- Progressive memory loss
- Personality changes
- Intellectual decline
- Losing interest in activities
- Sleep disturbances

Risk factors:
- Family history (in twenty percent of cases)
- Advanced age
- Head trauma
- Down's Syndrome (may have early onset of Alzheimer's)

Usual treatment:
- Medications (may temporarily improve memory, but does not halt disease)
- Support and education of family
- Patients often need nursing home placement as disease progresses

Usual course: Progressive and degenerative ending in death, generally within eight to ten years; at the beginning, symptoms may be mild with only loss of recent memory and inability to learn new information. This stage is followed by the need for assistance with activities of daily living (ADLs). In the severe or final stages, there is the inability to walk or perform any ADLs, resulting in complete dependence.

Spiritual considerations:
- Families have difficulty coping with this disease. As people with AD become more and more debilitated, they often forget their loved ones' names. Provide assurance and support for the family. Nursing home placement is often necessary for safety and better care. Recommend a facility that has a unit specializing in caring for people with AD.
- Encourage family members to arrange for durable power of attorney and advance directives as soon as possible (in preparation for the time when the person is no longer able to make independent decisions).
- Encourage the family to attend an AD support group. These groups often meet in local churches. Consider starting such a group in your own community if there is an identified need.

Suggested scriptures: Psalms 40: 16–17; Philippians 4:8

Resources:
Alzheimer's Association
919 N. Michigan Ave., Suite 1000
Chicago, IL
1–800–272–3900

Alzheimer's Disease International
www.alz.co.uk/

Amyotropic Lateral Sclerosis (ALS; commonly known as Lou
Gehrig's Disease)
Description: A progressive, degenerative disease of unknown cause that affects the nervous system, involving the brain and spinal cord. Degeneration progresses to total paralysis and the inability to breathe, leading to death. The person's sensory function is not affected.

Incidence: Rare (up to five per100,000 in the US); rare under age forty; increases with age

Prevalence: Males equally with females

Signs and symptoms:
- Muscle weakness (starting in the upper extremities)
- Trouble swallowing
- Trouble talking
- Trouble walking

Risk factors:
- Family history
- Age over forty

Usual treatment: Medications (though none are effective in halting the progression); support and education (emotional, spiritual, psychological counseling)

Usual course: Death usually occurs in two to five years after diagnosis; death occurs more rapidly if the lower brain is involved early in the course of the disease (difficulty swallowing may indicate this involvement).

Spiritual considerations:
- This disease is difficult for the person who has it and the family. There is no cure, and death is usually from respiratory or kidney failure.
- The person generally remains alert, oriented, and in full possession of their senses until the end, even though the body wastes away. The need for spiritual support is enormous, as people in a dependent state will have a lot of time to think about their situation. Many people will grapple with deep spiritual issues such as "why did God let this happen to me?"
- Provide spiritual and emotional support for the patient and

family through the entire course of the disease. The person will eventually be homebound. Make frequent visits.
- A few cases of longer life span or remission of the disease have been reported, but this outcome is rare.

Suggested scriptures: Psalms 37:3– 5; Psalms 27; Psalms 23; Revelations 21: 1–4

Resources: For an insider's view of ALS, read *Tuesdays with Morrie* by Mitch Albom (published by Doubleday and available at most local bookstores).

The Muscular Dystrophy Association
1–800–572–1717

Cerebral Palsy (CP)

Description: Motor disorders characterized by impaired voluntary movement caused by injury to the brain (resulting from lack of oxygen) of an infant or child, before, after, or during the birth process.

Incidence: 2.1 per 1,000 live births

Prevalence: Males equally with females

Signs and symptoms:
- Varies depending on type
- Floppiness
- Spastic muscles
- May have normal intelligence or some mental retardation

Risk factors: Problems during mother's pregnancy or at delivery

Usual treatment: Therapy (intense physical, occupational and speech therapy); monitoring throughout life for complications

Usual course: A chronic problem but not progressive; may result in significant disability

Spiritual considerations:
- Parents of children who have CP will need continued emotional and spiritual support.
- Some children will be wheelchair-bound. Mental retardation can occur with CP as well. Educate the faith community about the disease and special needs of the child.
- Provide hope that this is not a progressive disease and that therapy has been shown to improve function over time.

Suggested scriptures: Psalms 139: 1–18; Psalms 84: 11–12; Jeremiah 29: 11

Resources:
United Cerebral Palsy Associations
80 Maiden Lane, 8th Floor
New York, NY 10038–4811
212–683–6700
1–877–835–7335
www.ucpa.org

Down's Syndrome

Description: Down's syndrome, caused by an extra chromosome contributed by the father, or mother, is one of the most common forms of mental retardation. (The father may be the carrier of this chromosomal defect.) Down's syndrome is sometimes accompanied by other birth defects, such as abnormalities of the heart.

Incidence: One in 1000 live births

Predominance: Males equally with females; occurs the same amount in all races

Signs and symptoms:
- Slanted eyes
- Larger tongue
- Smaller ears
- Heart murmur
- Delay in development
- Mentally slow (IQ usually forty to forty-five)

Risk factors: Risk increases with age of the mother at time of conception (dramatic increase in risk as mother ages beyond thirty-five years old); risk is higher if mother is the carrier (1:10) versus father (1:20).

Usual treatment:
- Thorough evaluation of the child
- Education of the family/parents

Usual course: Delays in normal development that affect language, understanding, and later ability to be independent; premature aging; often experiences heart and bowel problems; shortened life span to about fifty to sixty years; dementia (Alzheimer's) is common in later life

Spiritual considerations:
- Serious spiritual implications exist when physicians encourage testing for Down syndrome and provide the option of terminating the pregnancy if the child will be born with it. Most mothers are asked if they want to have an amniocentesis (a test that can reveal the extra chromosome) and whether or not they would consider an abortion if the child has Down's syndrome.
- Provide spiritual support for mothers who are older and pregnant, knowing that this risk for the child is greatly increased.
- Take an active part in being present while parents undergo testing and decision-making that try their faith.
- Encourage parents who do make the difficult decision to raise

a child with this disease that they are usually loving, friendly, and a blessing to many people.

Suggested scriptures: Psalms 73: 23–26

Resources:
National Down's Syndrome Congress
1–800–232–NDSC
www.nas.com/downsyn

Guillain Barré Syndrome (GBS)

Description: A neurological disease characterized by progressive, symmetrical paralysis beginning with the lower body; caused by inflammation and damage to the peripheral nerves; it usually begins 1–3 weeks after an infection, surgery, or an immunization.

Incidence: 1.7 in 100,000 (mortality rate about five percent)

Prevalence: Males and females equal; affects people of all ages and ethnic backgrounds

Signs and symptoms:
- Fatigue
- Weakness that leads to paralysis
- Weakness moving symmetrically up from the feet
- Abnormal feelings in the arms, legs, or face
- Rapid onset of symptoms
- Elevated protein levels in the spinal fluid
- Decreased reflexes as the disease progresses

Risk factors:
- History of an illness with a temperature one to three weeks before
- Has been known to occur after the flu vaccine or other immunizations

Usual treatment:
- Medications (daily IV immune globulin)
- Plasmapheresis ("washing" the blood to get rid of antibodies)

Usual course: Rapid onset and progression that are a medical emergency; impaired breathing can be fatal; after the acute phase, symptoms plateau, followed by a prolonged recovery phase which leaves disabling effects (in thirty percent of cases).

Spiritual considerations:
- Fear and anxiety are common during diagnostic time.
- Plasmapheresis treatments may be difficult and elicit fears of death.
- Persons may be completely paralyzed and dependent in the acute phase.
- Strengthen the spiritual support network for the person and surround him/her with prayer.

Suggested scriptures: Isaiah 26: 3–4; Proverbs 3: 5–6

Resources:
Guillain-Barré Syndrome (GBS) Foundation International
610–667–0131

Meningitis

Description: A potentially life-threatening infection of the brain and spinal fluid that can be caused by bacteria or a virus. Meningitis is transmissible from one person to another and may be epidemic. The most severe form is caused by a specific bacterium.

Incidence: Depends on type; bacterial: three to ten cases per 100,000; viral: more than 10,000 cases per year

Prevalence: Males equally with females; viral is most common in young adults; bacterial is most common in those with weakened immune systems, infants, and elderly; Navajo Indian and American Eskimo may be more susceptible to bacterial type

Signs and symptoms:
- Fever
- Headache
- Stiff neck
- Nausea and vomiting
- Occasional rash

Risk factors:
- Impaired immune system
- Epidemics (where the bacteria become much stronger by infecting many people)

Usual treatment:
- Medications (appropriate antibiotics for the bacterial type)
- Hospitalization
- Rest

Usual course: Good prognosis with proper treatment, though there is a risk of death even with treatment; with viral type, recovery is usually complete within days to one week; however, the bacterial disease can progress very rapidly, leading to death within forty-eight hours from onset, so early diagnosis and treatment are essential.

Spiritual considerations:
- Viral meningitis is becoming more common on college campuses. This is a scary diagnosis for any parent of a child to hear, but provide hope that with prompt treatment, it is generally short-term.
- Provide comfort and a healing presence for the person and family while treatment is being administered.
- Prayer and fostering hope are most appropriate while waiting for improvement.

Suggested scriptures: Psalms 57:1; James 1:1–5

Resources:
www.meningitis.org
www.musa.org

Migraines

Description: A severe headache that may last from hours to days and is caused by sudden dilation of arteries in and around the brain. These headaches are episodic and can be triggered by allergies, stress, fatigue or even certain foods. They may be generalized or just on one side of the head.

Incidence: Females more than males in adults

Prevalence: May start in childhood and continue through adulthood

Signs and symptoms:
- Irritability
- Fatigue
- Headache
- Visual disturbances
- Nausea
- Vomiting
- Sensitivity to light
- Dizziness
- Muscle soreness

Risk factors:
- Family history
- Alcohol
- Emotional stress
- Young age
- Female
- Menstrual cycle

- Certain eating habits
- Emotional stress
- Allergies

Usual treatment:
- Sleep (lying down in a calm, dark, quiet place)
- Cold cloth to head or neck
- Avoid foods that may cause symptoms
- Avoid stress
- Medications (prompt use of vasoconstrictor medications may stop the migraine and should be continuously available)

Usual course: Most symptoms go away within seventy-two hours; as a person gets older, attacks are usually less frequent and not as severe.

Spiritual considerations:
- People sometimes judge those with migraines as having emotional rather than physical problems. Avoid judgmental attitudes about the cause of a person's migraines, and realize these severe headaches can be disabling to them. Provide compassion and understanding; teach congregational members to do the same.
- Instill hope that there is treatment and that attacks do pass.

Suggested scriptures: Psalms 23

Resources: www.migraines.org

Multiple sclerosis (MS)
Description: Degeneration of the myelin sheath of the nerves in patches in the brain and spinal cord; damage is due to inflammation with an unknown cause; commonly progressive and relapsing; the symptoms are varied and often vague.

Incidence: relatively common (25,000 new cases each year in the US)

Prevalence: Females more than males; major cause of disability in young adults (ages sixteen to forty); affects Anglo-Americans more than African-Americans or Asian-Americans

Signs and symptoms:
- Visual problems
- Fatigue
- Bladder problems
- Poor coordination
- Difficulty walking
- Mood swings
- Weakness

Risk factors:
- Living in a cooler northern climate
- Being of European descent
- Family history

Usual treatment:
- Medication (cortisone medications in acute episodes and subcutaneous injections of interferons for long-term management)
- Treat acute episodes
- Rest and build endurance

Usual course: Varies according to type of MS, but highly unpredictable; a chronic disorder with no cure, though life span is not shortened for most people

Spiritual considerations:
- Fatigue is a major problem.
- Disease is often progressive and associated with recurring feelings of sorrow.
- Offer hope—new treatments have shown great promise.
- Foster spiritual support network.

Suggested scriptures: Isaiah 35: 3–4; Isaiah 40: 31

Resources:
National Multiple Sclerosis Society
733 3rd Avenue, 6th Floor
New York, NY 10017
1–800–Fight MS (1–800–344–4867)
http:www.nationalmssociety.org
info@nmss.org

Myasthenia Gravis (MG)

Description: A disorder in which messages are not conducted properly between the nerves and muscles, resulting in muscle fatigue and weakness because the signals are blocked. This disease is commonly heralded by weakness of the eye lids, causing them to droop.

Incidence: Three per100,000 in the US

Predominance: Females more than males; diagnosed most often between ages twenty and forty

Signs and symptoms:
- Droopy eyelids
- Double vision
- Weakness
- Fatigue
- Trouble swallowing and chewing

Risk factors:
- Females ages twenty to forty
- Family history

Usual treatment:
- Medication (to prevent formation of substances in the body that block the nerve conduction to the muscles)

- Continued monitoring (exacerbations often require hospital-ization)
- Surgery in some cases (remove thymus gland)
- Plasmapheresis (to cleanse the blood plasma)

Usual course: Varies greatly; chronic and characterized by remissions and exacerbations that can be mild to life-threatening. The exacerbation may last hours to days. Disease may progress to partial paralysis of the arms and legs and even the respiratory muscles to cause death.

Spiritual considerations:
- People with MG are often dependent upon medication for the duration of their lives..
- Since patients are mainly women of childbearing age, the faith community should make child care a priority. This disease can be discouraging. Flare-ups can even result in being put on a ventilator. Provide a hopeful, calm and supportive environment. Plan to visit the hospital frequently and help the family cope during these times. Let the person and family know that they are not alone.

Suggested scriptures: Lamentations 3: 22–26

Resources:
Myasthenia Gravis Foundation
5481 Cedar Lake Road, Suite 204
Minneapolis, MN 55416
1–800–541–5454
www.myasthenia.org

Parkinson's Disease (PD)
Description: A slowly progressive degenerative central nervous system disorder characterized by slow movements, muscle rigidity, resting tremor, and gait instability. There is a depletion of dopamine in the brain, but the cause is unknown.

Incidence: Common (more than one million in US; 50,000 new cases per year; one in every 100 persons after age fifty-five)

Prevalence: Males more than females

Signs and symptoms:
- Stiffness (rigidity)
- Slowness of movement (bradykinesia)
- Tremor
- Depression
- Dementia
- Gait disturbances
- Bladder and sexual dysfunction

Risk factors: Unknown

Usual treatment:
- Medication (that provides chemical dopamine to the brain)
- Support/education
- Surgical intervention (to destroy areas of the brain that cause muscle rigidity)
- Fetal tissue implants have shown some success in reducing spasticity and rigidity

Usual course: A chronic disorder with no cure; can ultimately lead to being bedridden and death

Spiritual considerations:
- Disease is progressive and associated with continued feelings of sorrow.
- Family and person may be grieving multiple losses—offer comfort.
- Family and especially spouse or caregiver will require long-term spiritual and emotional support.
- Medication management is lifelong, and the person with PD is quite dependent on medication to maintain physical activity

Suggested scriptures: Isaiah 35: 3–10; Psalm 118

Resources:
National Parkinson Foundation
1501 N. W. Ninth Avenue
Miami, FL 33136
1–800–327–4545
http://www.Parkinson.org

Parkinson's Disease Foundation
1–800–457–6676
http://www.pdf.org
info@pdf.org

Seizures (also called Seizure Disorders or Epilepsy)
Description: Seizures are alterations in consciousness or neurological function related to abnormal electrical impulses in the brain. There are several types, including epilepsy, and numerous possible causes. However, fifty percent of all cases are of unknown cause.

Incidence: Common (1.5 million in the US experience seizure)

Prevalence: Males equally with females; occurs in all age groups

Signs and symptoms:
- Vary, depending on type but may include:
- Muscle contractions
- Loss of consciousness or altered consciousness
- Being unaware of surroundings
- Fever (in young children)
- Headache
- In severe cases, breathing may stop

Risk factors:
- Certain brain disorders
- Head injury or stroke

- Genetics
- Low blood sugar
- High fever
- Infections
- Use of certain drugs

Usual treatment:
- Medication (anticonvulsants and medications to treat the cause)
- Monitoring

Usual course: Varies, depending on the type. First line drug therapy eliminates seizures in 1/3 and greatly reduces seizures in another 1/3. For those patients whose seizures are not controlled with first line medications, more complex medications are available. The first line drugs have fewer side effects and require less monitoring than the complex medications and therefore are preferred.

Spiritual considerations:
- A condition called status epilepticus (repeated seizures that go on for a long period of time) is a medical emergency. Seek emergency treatment.
- This is a scary condition. If someone in your congregation has epilepsy or problems with seizures, educate your staff and congregation on how to help. Encourage the person to comply with treatment, as medications can help control seizures in most cases. Have an emergency plan in place.
- Provide hope that this problem can be controlled with proper treatment. Address fears and anxiety. Strengthen spiritual support systems.

Suggested scriptures: Philippians 4:19; Philippians 4: 6–7

Resources:
Epilepsy Foundation of America
www.efa.org

Shingles *(Herpes Zoster)*

Description: A painful disorder caused by a reactivated varicella virus (the same virus causing chicken pox) that erupts along the path of a sensory nerve. After an episode of chicken pox, the virus remains dormant in the *ganglia* of the central nervous system. For unknown reasons, the virus becomes activated, causing inflammatory changes in the nerve attached to the infected ganglia, resulting in blister-like eruptions and neuralgic pain that follows the path of that nerve.

Incidence: Common (ten to twenty percent of Americans will have shingles at some point in their lives)

Prevalence: Most common among those over age sixty-five and those with impaired immune systems

Signs and symptoms:
- Blister-like lesions along the course of the involved nerve. The lesions of *herpes zoster* always stop at the mid-line of the body and never occur bilaterally.
- Pain

Risk factors:
- Advanced age
- Impaired immunity

Usual treatment:
- Antiviral medications
- Rest

Usual course: Pain along the course of a spinal nerve is the first symptom and is often severe. This pain may last two to three days before the skin lesions appear. Lesions usually continue to form, and long-lasting pain may occur even after the lesions are healed. Fewer than four percent of people with shingles experience recurrence. It sometimes recurs in people with decreased immunity; recurrences may also be associated with extreme emotional stress.

Spiritual considerations:
- Any person who has had the chicken pox can get shingles. Since the same virus causes both, people with either problem should not be around children or older people, nor work in the nursery at church until they are completely well.
- Provide hope. While shingles may be painful and uncomfortable, it is highly treatable and usually a short-term problem.
- Encourage stress management, prayer, and use of spiritual support systems while the disorder is active. In the contagious phase, congregational members may opt to provide phone calls, cards or deliver meals.

Suggested scriptures: Psalms 37: 23–24; Psalms 73: 26

Resources:
Visiting Nurses Association web site
www.aftershingles.com

Spinal cord injury (SCI)
Description: Spinal cord injury may consist of a bruise (contusion), which will improve as swelling subsides, or compression (which causes more lasting paralysis and weakness), or deep tearing (laceration or transection) of the spinal cord, which causes permanent loss of spinal cord function below the level of the injury and, therefore, complete paralysis and loss of feeling from the level of injury down. These injuries are usually caused by trauma such as motor vehicle or sports-related accidents.

Incidence: Common

Prevalence: Most common among males age fifteen to middle adulthood

Signs and symptoms:
- Loss of feeling and movement below the level of the injury
- Loss of ability to control bodily functions below the level of the injury

Risk factors: engaging in high-risk activities that could injure the neck or back

Usual treatment:
- Stabilizing the spine through surgery and/or braces
- Medications to manage complications (such as infections and muscle spasms)
- Extensive rehabilitation

Usual course: Symptoms vary with incomplete injuries (that is, spinal cord not severed). If the spinal cord is only mildly bruised, numbness and or weakness or even paralysis of the arms or legs may occur temporarily—for how long depends on the severity of the contusion. Some incomplete injuries may result in sufficient destruction of the spinal cord to cause permanent loss of function of the arms, legs, or both.

Spiritual considerations:
- This is a problem of devastating magnitude that affects the entire family and community.
- The injured person and family members often deal with feelings of guilt, anger, loss, and grief.
- Thoughts of suicide may occur to people with permanent paralysis.
- SCI places an enormous strain on marital or intimate relationships, which often change after the accident. Provide as much social, economic, and spiritual support as possible, and plan for the long-term.
- Peer support has been shown to help. Help link the person and family with another person that has successfully dealt with the same kind of injury.

- For injuries high in the spinal cord ("broken necks"), the person may be dependent on a ventilator for the rest of his or her life.
- Most SCI patients are wheelchair-bound; transportation and access to buildings is often a concern; make sure your church is accessible and has bathroom facilities to accommodate wheelchairs.

Suggested scriptures: Psalms 69: 14–17; Romans 8: 18

Resources:
Midwest Regional Spinal Cord Injury Care System
250 E. Superior, Room 619
Chicago, IL 60611
312–908–3425

National Spinal Cord Injury Association
600 W. Cummings Park, Suite 2000
Woburn, MA 01801

Stroke (also called Cerebrovascular Accident (CVA) or Brain Attack)

Description: An interruption in the blood supply to the brain caused by blocking of an artery, or rupture of a blood vessel in the brain that causes bleeding into the tissue

Incidence: At least 500,000–600,000 new cases each year in the US

Prevalence: Males more than females until menopause, then nearly equal; risk increases with age

Signs and symptoms:
- Headache
- Numbness or tingling in face or extremities
- Weakness or paralysis on one side of body
- Slurred speech

- Visual deficits
- Dizziness
- Loss of consciousness

Risk factors:
- Advanced age
- High blood pressure
- Heart disease
- Smoking
- Diabetes
- Heredity

Usual treatment:
- Medication (clot-busting medication may be given for stroke caused by a clot, but only within a three-hour window from onset of symptoms, so early treatment is essential)
- Surgery (if indicated for blockage or hemorrhage)
- Rehabilitation (for reeducation and training)
- Lifestyle modifications (lose weight, stop smoking, control high blood pressure, reduce or eliminate alcohol intake)

Usual course: Recovery time varies (depending on location and severity of the stroke); stroke may leave long-lasting effects. The effects of stroke vary from complete recovery of function to permanent paralysis to coma or death—again, depending on the location and extent of damage within the brain.

Spiritual considerations:
- People may be left with severe physical and cognitive deficits that require an extensive period of rehabilitation
- Stroke affects the entire family
- Stroke survivors report that prayer, faith, hope, positive thinking, and humor are good coping strategies

Suggested scriptures: Psalms 103: 5; Philippians 4:13

Resources:
National Stroke Association
300 East Hampden Ave., Suite 240
Englewood, CO 80110–2622
www.nsa.org

GASTROINTESTINAL AND OTHER ORGAN PROBLEMS (STOMACH, INTESTINES, BOWELS, AND OTHER INTERNAL ORGANS)

Crohn's Disease

Description: A chronic and progressive condition involving inflammation of the wall of the bowel involving mainly the lower part of the small bowel and colon, but may occur in any part of the stomach or intestines. The cause is unknown. Inflammation progresses to ulceration and swelling of the bowel with permanent scarring and narrowing.

Incidence: Twenty to100 per 100,000 in the US

Prevalence: Females more than males; Anglo-Americans more than African-Americans or Asian-Americans; more common among Jews; usually diagnosed between fifteen and twenty-five years of age

Signs and symptoms:
- Diarrhea
- Abdominal pain
- Weight loss
- Intestinal obstruction

Risk factors:
- Cigarette smoking
- Family history

Usual treatment:
- Medication (for reducing inflammation)

- Surgery
- Ongoing monitoring

Usual course: The symptoms usually appear and then become chronic; however, the onset may be sudden, with pain in the abdomen suggesting appendicitis. Although spontaneous remission or medical therapy may result in a prolonged time with no symptoms, cure of the disease is rare. Intermittent exacerbations are usual, but disease-related mortality is rare. People with Crohn's disease of the small bowel are at greater risk for small bowel cancer.

Spiritual considerations:
- Because this is a chronic disorder, strengthen social and spiritual support networks.
- Be aware that a person with this disorder may undergo numerous surgeries throughout the course of the disease. Have a plan to assist the person and family during these times, and plan for hospital visits.

Scripture verses: Psalms 139

Resources:
Crohn's and Colitis Foundation of America Inc.
11th Floor
386 Park Avenue South
New York, NY 10016
1–800–343–3637
www.ccfa.org
info@ccfa.org
www.niddk.nih.gov/health/digest/pubs/crohns/crohns.htm

Hepatitis

Description: The main causes of hepatitis are a group of viruses called *Hepatitis A, B, and C,* which infect the liver. Although these are all forms of hepatitis, they are widely different diseases with different modes of transmission and courses. *Hepatitis A* is an acute-onset illness acquired by ingesting contaminated material usually by hand to mouth or by eating food contaminated by the virus. *Hepatitis B* occurs from contact with an infected person's blood, as can happen when drug addicts share needles. Health care workers are at risk for catching this form of hepatitis because they come in contact with patient's blood. *Hepatitis C* is contracted mainly by receiving a contaminated blood transfusion or by IV drug use. *Hepatitis B* and *C* do not have acute onset but develop as weakness, loss of appetite and jaundice. *Hepatitis C* is totally silent, gradually destroying the liver without symptoms.

Incidence: Common; can be acute or chronic

Prevalence: Males more than females; different age groups depending on the type

Signs and symptoms:
- Fever
- Nausea
- Anorexia
- Jaundice
- Fatigue
- Dark urine
- Abdominal pain

Risk factors:
- Health care workers and IV drug users are at risk
- Needle sticks with contaminated needles
- Transfusions with contaminated blood
- Sexual relations with an infected person
- Dialysis

Usual treatment:
- Medication
- Lifestyle changes (proper diet; good hygiene; safe sex; proper needle disposal)

- Sometimes surgery (liver transplant)

Usual course: *Hepatitis A* begins like other viral illnesses with aches and pains, followed by vomiting and jaundice. Recovery usually leaves no lasting liver injury and is most often complete within two to three weeks. *Hepatitis B* has a more gradual onset, but lets its presence be known by loss of appetite, weakness, and jaundice. After a few weeks or a few months, many patients with *Hepatitis B* recover. However, some patients develop chronic hepatitis that continues gradually destroying the liver, leading to liver failure and death. *Hepatitis C* is usually totally silent. Diagnosis is made by blood tests that reveal liver abnormalities, followed by a specific blood test for *Hepatitis C*. The disease sometimes becomes inactive but generally leads to destruction of the liver and death. Cancer of the liver is much more common in patients with chronic *Hepatitis B & C*.

Spiritual considerations:
- This diagnosis carries some fear and stigma, since some of the causes are related to alternative lifestyles which may not be acceptable in certain faith communities. Provide understanding for each person, and education for congregation members.
- Promote hope that the disease will be treatable.
- Prayer and positive thinking may be helpful.

Suggested scriptures: Psalms 100; Psalms 103: 2–5

Resources: www.cdc.gov/ncidod/diseases/hepatitis/a/index.htm

Irritable Bowel Syndrome (IBS)
Description: A disorder involving the entire GI (gastrointestinal, or stomach and intestines) tract which causes altered bowel function with abdominal pain, increased gas, and diarrhea or constipation.

Incidence: Unknown, but common among adults and does tend to run in families

Prevalence: Females more than males (2:1) in the US; males more than females in other countries; seen most often among those in their late twenties through thirties.

Signs and symptoms:
- Abdominal pain
- Mucus in stools
- Urgency with bowel movements
- Constipation
- Diarrhea

Risk factors:
- Family history of bowel disorders
- History of sexual abuse

Usual treatment:
- Reduce stress
- Avoid large meals
- Avoid spicy, fried and fatty foods
- Avoid milk products
- Take medication

Usual course: Occurs with stress or with the ingestion of certain foods. It is most often a chronic condition that seems to improve with advanced age. It does not progress into cancer or other disease. Progression or improvement of the disorder often corresponds to the status of stress, anxiety, or mood disorders.

Spiritual considerations:
- Provide a calm and supportive environment.
- Be aware that some people who have this disorder have been victims of sexual or other physical abuse and may need spiritual counseling to deal with underlying issues.
- When making a church facility accessible be sure to have restroom facilities on each level, located in a convenient place.

- Encourage the person to find a physician who will have sympathetic understanding of this disorder.

Suggested scriptures: 1 Thessalonians 5: 16–24

Resources: http//:www.aboutibs.org

Pancreatitis

Description: Inflammation of the pancreas that can be acute or chronic. The pancreas, located in the upper abdomen, is involved in the digestive process as well in as the manufacture of insulin. The inflammation can originate from several sources—such as obstruction of the pancreatic duct by gallstones, viral infections, or the ingestion of alcohol. When pancreatic inflammation occurs, digestive enzymes are released into the blood stream. Pancreatitis can also occur with no apparent cause.

Incidence: Ten to twenty-two per100,000 in the US

Prevalence: Males equally to females; chronic pancreatitis occurs more often in middle aged adults and is usually related to alcohol abuse

Signs and symptoms:
- Abdominal pain
- Nausea
- Vomiting
- Fever
- Mild jaundice

Risk factors:
- Certain medications
- Alcohol abuse
- Lupus
- AIDS

- Infections
- Other diseases

Usual treatment:
- Medication (antibiotics and pain control)
- Surgery in some cases
- Rest
- Special diet
- Eliminate alcohol use
- Fluid replacement in severe cases

Usual course: Acute pancreatitis usually begins suddenly with the onset of severe abdominal pain when it originates from gallstones, infection, or unknown cause. Alcoholic pancreatitis has a more gradual onset. Uncontrollable vomiting accompanies the pain as does heavy sweating and high fever, as well as rapid pulse and often low blood pressure. Death may occur in the first several days in severe cases, especially in cases where there is death of pancreatic tissue and hemorrhage. Most cases of pancreatitis are not severe, and recovery is complete in one to two weeks. Chronic pancreatitis is characterized by multiple episodes that recur over the years.

Spiritual considerations:
- Fear and anxiety are common in the diagnosis phase. Provide comfort.
- Foster hope that things will improve, and encourage person to stick with the medical plan prescribed.

Suggested scriptures: Psalm 107

Resources: www.cdc.gov

Peptic Ulcer Disease
Description: Peptic ulcer disease means ulceration in the stomach or the first segment of the small intestine leading from the stomach *(duodenum)*. These areas are exposed to enzymes and acid manufac-

tured by the stomach. The acid produced is involved in the development of ulcers. Other factors also lead to ulceration by reducing the lining of the stomach and the duodenum's defense and repair mechanisms, allowing the acid to erode the lining and cause ulcerations. The main causes of peptic ulcer disease are an infection by a bacterium (H. Pylori) or frequent use of medications taken for pain or arthritis (Ibuprofen® and similar anti-inflammatory medication).

Incidence: Males about equally to females

Prevalence: More often in adults

Signs and symptoms:
• Burning type of stomach pain (worse a couple of hours after meals)
• Belching
• Bloating
• In more severe cases:
• Nausea
• Vomiting
• Severe pain
• Weight loss
• Black stools or vomited blood

Risk factors:
• Family history
• Cigarette smoking
• Certain drugs (NSAIDS—non-steroidal anti-inflammatory drugs used for arthritis and pain, such as Ibuprofen®)
• Stress
• Lower socioeconomic status

Usual treatment:
• Medication (highly effective in restoring the defenses in the lining in the stomach.

- Lifestyle changes (manage stress, stop smoking, proper diet, avoid alcohol)

Usual course: Usually good prognosis with proper treatment. Excellent results have been seen with the use of the new anti-ulcer medications. Healing of the ulcer most often occurs within two weeks. If ulcers erode a blood vessel, massive, life-threatening hemorrhage can occur, and emergency medical care is necessary. If the bacterium H. Pylori is left untreated, ulcerations will continue to occur until it is eradicated by the use of antibiotics. Continuous use of Ibuprofen® type drugs can also lead to recurrent ulcerations.

Spiritual considerations:
- Provide emotional and spiritual support.
- May need diagnostic tests (such as endoscopy). Visits or physical presence at this time would be comforting to the person and family.

Suggested scriptures: Lamentations 3: 22–26

Resources: www.cdc.gov/ulcer

REPRODUCTIVE, SEXUAL, AND URINARY CONDITIONS

Ectopic Pregnancy

Description: The condition occurs when the fertilized egg implants outside of the uterus. The most common location for this to occur is in the Fallopian tubes, though it may implant in the abdomen, outside the uterus, or on an ovary. This condition is incompatible with the life of the fetus and may pose a threat to the pregnant woman.

Incidence: Not uncommon (one in fifty pregnancies) in women of childbearing age

Signs and symptoms:
- Early signs of pregnancy (breast tenderness, nausea, missed period)
- Irregular vaginal bleeding
- Lower abdominal pain, usually on one side
- Rupture with bleeding inside the abdomen
- May progress to severe pelvic pain, shoulder pain, nausea,
- vomiting, dizziness

Risk Factors:
- Previous ectopic pregnancy
- Sexually transmitted disease
- Fertility drugs
- Endometriosis
- Smoking
- Damaged fallopian tubes (including previous tubal surgery)

Usual treatment:
- Surgery
- Medication (methotrexate for first six weeks)

Usual course: This condition occurs early in pregnancy, usually within the initial four to six weeks and often before pregnancy has been diagnosed. Irregular vaginal bleeding may occur first, but it is the appearance of abdominal pain that indicates the presence of the problem. The condition ends when the diagnosis is made and appropriate treatment (usually surgery) is instituted, but the emotional effects may linger.

Spiritual considerations:
- Acknowledge loss and allow the natural course of the grieving process for both partners.
- Encourage the use of self-help groups.
- Support use of coping strategies such as prayer, meditation, and relaxation.

Suggested scriptures: Jeremiah 17: 7–8

Resources:
March of Dimes Birth Defects Foundation
1275 Mamaroneck Avenue
White Plains, NY 10605
888–MODIMES (663–4637)
www.modimes.org/healthlibrary2/FactSheets/Ectopic_and_Molar.htm

Genital Herpes (Herpes Simplex Virus –HSV)
Description: The cold sore or fever blister is a common occurrence, and everyone is familiar with its appearance. It is caused by the Herpes Simplex Virus. Similar lesions can occur on the genitalia. *Herpes I* and *Herpes II* were originally thought to be two different types of viruses, *type I* infecting the lips and *type II* infecting the genitalia. Though there *are* two different types of viruses, *type I* may also infect the lip. After initial infection, both types of herpes simplex remain in the body permanently and are incurable. Recurrent lesions occur, often precipitated by exposure to sunlight, illness with fever, or stress. The eruptions can occur anywhere on the skin. *HSV II* usually causes genital herpes and can be transmitted by direct sexual contact.

Incidence: Common (sixty million Americans; eighty percent of Americans have oral herpes, or "cold sores")

Prevalence: Female (the infection can be passed on to the newborn if exposure to active sores occurs during delivery)

Signs and symptoms:
• Itching, burning in genital or anal regions
• Pain in genital area, legs or buttocks
• Vaginal discharge
• Abdominal pressure
• Blisters and open sores (mouth, penis, vagina)
• Fever

- Headache
- Muscle aches
- Painful urination
- Swollen glands in groin area

Risk factors:
- Age (less than twenty-five years of age)
- Unprotected sex (though this disease can also spread without sex)
- Having many sexual partners

Usual treatment:
- Medication (antiviral)
- Site treatment of sores
- Avoidance of sexual contact until sores have completely healed, then use condoms

Usual course: The lesions heal on their own in eight to twelve days but recurrence may be frequent, especially if illness, fatigue, or stress, weaken the immune system. Treatment with antiviral agents reduces incidence of relapse. Although herpes simplex is not curable, it poses little threat to normal life.

Spiritual considerations:
- Promote exploration of feelings, which may include anger, guilt, blame, and sadness
- Instill hope
- Encourage use of self-help groups

Suggested scriptures: Psalm 142: 6a; Psalms 1: 1–3

Resources:
American Social Health Association
P.O. Box 13827
Research Triangle Park, NC 27709
(919) 361–8400

Infertility

Description: Infertility is the failure to achieve pregnancy despite a couple's efforts. How long a couple may try to conceive before doctors determine infertility varies, most specialists saying as little as one year, but others say as many as five. On average, ovulation occurs twelve times per year (once per month). The period of fertility for each cycle may be four to five days or less, and so a woman may not become pregnant simply because the couple misses the fertile period. But when a number of periods have occurred without resulting in pregnancy, infertility is considered to exist. There are many causes of infertility: the most common causes are insufficient sperm count, failure to ovulate, or disease of the fallopian tubes that provides a barrier and prevents the sperm from meeting the egg.

Incidence: Common (six million Americans; ten percent of the population at reproductive age)

Prevalence: Equally among males and females

Signs and symptoms:
• One year of unprotected intercourse without conception

Risk factors:
• Smoking
• Alcohol and drugs
• Environmental toxins
• Pesticides
• Lead
• Female hormone imbalance
• Blocked fallopian tubes
• Pelvic inflammatory disease
• Endometriosis
• Severe medical illnesses (mumps)
• STD (sexually transmitted disease)
• Injury to testicles or impaired function
• Diabetes

Usual treatment (depends on cause):
- Medications (to stimulate ovulation)
- Surgery
- Utilize reproductive technologies to relieve problems in the reproductive process, such as failure to ovulate, blocked tubes or low sperm count.

Usual course: Varies; some infertility problems are permanent. However, every effort to identify the cause should be made so that pregnancy can be achieved.

Spiritual considerations:
- This situation may cause strain in a marital relationship; discuss ways partners can support each other.
- Be aware that the couple may experience isolation, grief, and depression.
- Instill hope.

Suggested scriptures: Psalms 37: 3–7; Lamentations 3: 24–26

Resources:
RESOLVE: National Infertility Association
1310 Broadway
Somerville, MA 02144
(617) 623–0744

Impotence (Erectile Dysfunction)
Description: The inability to achieve or maintain a penile erection for sexual intercourse. This problem can accompany diseases such as diabetes and prostate disorders. Psychological problems may also cause or contribute to this disorder.

Incidence: Common (thirty million Americans)

Prevalence: Males

Signs and symptoms:
- Inability to achieve an erection (occasional or always)
- Inability to maintain erection

Risk factors:
- Surgery or trauma (spinal cord injury)
- Medications
- Diseases and disorders (diabetes, chronic illnesses)
- Substance abuse
- Stress, depression, anxiety

Usual treatment:
- Medication (Viagra®—to dilate the artery that supplies blood to the penis, thereby facilitating erection)
- Counseling
- Surgery (installation of penile prosthesis)
- Blood is drawn into the penis by the use of a vacuum

Usual course: Varies. When erectile dysfunction accompanies certain diseases, it is often permanent. Viagra® has offered new hope and helps many men achieve erection. Certain medications can cause impotence; when these medications are discontinued, erection is restored. Treatment of any existing prostate infections may also improve erectile dysfunction.

Spiritual considerations:
- Loss and grief can have a devastating effect on the sexual desire and the erectile ability of the male. Impotence, in turn, can bring on anxiety which further complicates the impotence. Encourage person to explore feelings associated with this condition.
- Use of coping strategies such as prayer, meditation, and relaxation can help to decrease anxiety.

Suggested scriptures: Proverbs 3: 5–6

Resources:
National Kidney and Urologic Diseases Information Clearinghouse
Office of Communications and Public Liaison
NIDDK, NIH
31 Center Drive, MSC 2560
Bethesda, MD 20892–2560

Menopause

Description: Menopause occurs when the ovaries no longer manufacture estrogen and is a natural consequence of aging. Menopause
is considered to be complete when twelve consecutive menstrual
periods have been missed. Menopause may occur abruptly when the
ovaries are surgically removed.

Incidence: Common (36 million American women); usually happens between ages forty-five and sixty

Prevalence: Females

Signs and symptoms:
- Hot flashes and night sweats
- Disrupted sleep
- Fatigue
- Increased sweating
- Mood swings
- Vaginal dryness
- Thinning and decreased elasticity of skin
- Urinary incontinence
- Loss of, or decrease in, sex drive

Risk factors:
- Age
- Surgical removal of ovaries

Usual treatment:
- Hormone replacement therapy

- Increase use of soy products in diet
- Alternative complementary medication

Usual course: Many women become menopausal without any symptoms and others have symptoms. Many psychoemotional changes are attributed to the menopause such as mood shifts and emotional instability, but there is no scientific evidence to suggest that mental processes are connected to the presence or absence of estrogen. Abrupt surgical menopause is rarely associated with psychological symptoms.

Spiritual considerations:
- Feminine identity and recognition of aging (loss of youth) may be issues for some women.
- Relationships, especially with the sexual partner, may be strained.

Suggested scriptures: Psalm 145:15–21; Proverbs 16:31; 1 Samuel 12:24

Resources:
National Institutes of Health
31 Center Drive, MSC 2560
Bethesda, MD 20892–2560

National Women's Health Information Center
8550 Arlington Blvd., Suite 300
Fairfax, VA 22031
800–994–WOMAN (800–994–9662)
www.4woman.gov/

Miscarriage

Description: Miscarriage is the spontaneous interruption of pregnancy. It is not a medical term but is often used because of the misunderstood implications of the appropriate medical term "spontaneous abortion." Pregnancy is separated into three phases: first, second, and third trimester. Miscarriage usually refers to interruption of pregnancy from natural causes in the first two trimesters. The most common cause of miscarriage is the body's rejection of fertilized, defective eggs. Third trimester miscarriage is usually caused by very different factors.

Incidence: Common (up to twenty percent of all pregnancies)

Prevalence: Women of childbearing age

Signs and symptoms:
- Vaginal bleeding that may include passing of tissue or clots
- Pelvic cramping
- Abdominal or lower back pain

Risk factors:
- Previous miscarriage
- STDs

Usual treatment:
- Rest
- No sex until physician permits
- Three month waiting period before trying to become pregnant
- Dilation and curettage (D & C) if miscarriage is incomplete and fetal tissue remains

Usual course: The event is much more common in the first six weeks of pregnancy and is terminated when the uterus is empty of fetal matter. The psychological impact of miscarriage can be severe. Surgery (D & C) is sometimes indicated to stop bleeding and prevent infection if the uterus still contains fetal tissue.

Spiritual considerations:
- Acknowledge the loss and allow the natural process of grieving for both partners.
- Encourage the use of self-help groups.

• Support the use of coping strategies such as prayer, meditation, and relaxation.

Suggested scriptures: 1 Corinthians 10:13; Lamentations 3:32–33; Psalms 34: 18

Resources:
National Women's Health Information Center
8550 Arlington Blvd., Suite 300
Fairfax, VA 22031
800–994–WOMAN (800–994–9662)
www.4woman.gov/

March of Dimes Birth Defects Foundation
1275 Mamaroneck Avenue
White Plains, NY 10605
888–MODIMES (663–4637)

Postpartum Depression

Description: Postpartum depression is more than the short term down mood that often accompanies childbirth. This condition may be experienced as severe, incapacitating depression, with episodes of psychosis. Postpartum depression is believed to be caused by a chemical imbalance. The major symptoms include mood change and extreme fatigue. These symptoms may even appear months after childbirth and can be severe. Other physical symptoms include headaches, palpitations, sleep disorders, abdominal pain, nausea and loss of appetite.

Incidence: Fairly common (with childbearing women); one in ten women

Prevalence: Females

Signs and symptoms: Symptoms are usually subtle at first and attributed to other conditions. See the section on Depression.

Risk factors:
- Childbirth
- History of depression
- Previous history of postpartum depression (fifty percent chance of recurrence with subsequent births)

Usual treatment:
- Medication (antidepressants)
- Psychotherapy, especially cognitive therapy
- Electroconvulsive therapy (ECT or "shock therapy")
- Complementary alternative medication

Usual course: The course of this illness often goes longer than it has to because patients often try to conceal their feelings, out of the belief that only a bad mother would have negative thoughts or emotional responses after having a baby. When women delay seeking help the condition gets worse. Medication and counseling will usually improve the condition within a few weeks. However, sometimes the depression becomes so severe that the person becomes completely unable to function and displays psychotic behavior.

Spiritual considerations:
- Keep in mind that a woman with postpartum depression is at risk for suicide (and homicide).
- Address feelings of helplessness and hopelessness. A woman with postpartum depression needs reassurance, since she may consider herself unworthy of attention.

Suggested scriptures: Psalm 127: 3–5

Resources: See the section on Depression

Sexually Transmitted Diseases (STDs)

Description: Sexually transmitted diseases are those passed from one person to another by some form of sexual contact. This group of diseases includes at least twenty types. They are highly contagious and often unreported. AIDS is the most serious STD. Syphilis, gonorrhea, and chlamydia are also common STDs.

Incidence: Common (fifteen million Americans per year)

Prevalence: Males and females affected at about the same rate

Signs and symptoms:
- Variable—often produce no symptoms, but the infected person can transmit illness to sexual partner
- Herpes Simplex Virus—painful ulcers on the skin of genitalia

Symptoms for Chlamydia and Gonorrhea
- Male: penile discharge, "burning" with urination
- Female: vaginal discharge

Symptoms for Syphilis
- Initially, nonpainful genital ulcers
- Later, painful joints, swollen lymph glands, neurological damage

Risk factors: Being less than twenty-five years of age

Usual treatment:
- Medication (appropriate antibiotics)
- Avoiding unprotected sexual contact with other people is key

Usual course: Varies, though many diseases respond well to medication. *AIDS* is extremely slow to develop (see section on *AIDS*).

Syphilis usually begins three to four weeks after exposure with a nonpainful ulcer on the genitalia. Untreated, this disease progresses, in six to twelve weeks, into the secondary stage with the appearance of characteristic rashes. During this stage, infection of lymph nodes occurs in many areas throughout the body. The third, or latent, stage follows: the disease may then seem dormant and may remain so for years. However, in three to ten years after the initial infection, abscess-like lesions develop in the skin, nose, and mouth. The heart and brain may eventually be affected. Appropriate treatment with antibiotics can stop this disease and prevent progression to the various stages.

Gonorrhea becomes evident in men by a yellowish-white discharge from the urethra. Diagnosis of the disease is usually made promptly. In women, the disease is not obvious. Many times, the infected person does not know she has it. The disease progresses with additional complications. The time from exposure to appearance of symptoms is two to fourteen days for men, and seven to twenty-one days for women. Left untreated, gonorrhea can spread to other sex organs and to other areas of the body. Gonorrheal arthritis is a fairly common result of untreated disease. Gonorrhea has become resistant to many of the antibiotics used in the past and is now much harder to eradicate.

Chlamydia is a bacteria that causes infection in both males and females. It can invade the tubes of the female or be confined to the vagina or the bladder. In the male the bacteria infects the urethra, the tube from the bladder.

Spiritual considerations:
 * Promote exploration of feelings, which may include anger, guilt, blame, and sadness.
 * Instill hope.
 * Encourage use of self-help groups.

Suggested scriptures: Psalm 103; 1 Corinthians 6: 19–20

Resources:
Center for Disease Control
National Center for HIV, STD, and TB Prevention
1108 Corporate Square
Atlanta, GA 30329
800–227–8922 (M-F 8 a.m.–11 p.m. EST)
cdc.gov.nchstp/dstd/disease_info.htm

National Women's Health Information Center
8550 Arlington Blvd., Suite 300
Fairfax, VA 22031
800–994–WOMAN (800–994–9662)
www.4woman.gov/

Urinary Incontinence

Description: A failure of the bladder support structures causes urine to pool in the *urethra,* the tube that empties the bladder. When pressure increases in the abdomen, as with coughing or sneezing, urine is forced from the bladder. If the condition progresses, incontinence may occur even as a result of walking up steps or of even mild lifting. Although bladder incontinence has marked social implications, it has no ill effects on a generally healthy person. Urinary tract infections may be more frequent due to the pooling of urine, but these infections are rarely severe.

Incidence: Common (twelve million Americans)

Prevalence: Females (one in every ten people more than sixty-five years of age)

Signs and symptoms:
- Leakage of urine
- Strong desire to urinate
- Bed-wetting/wetting while sleeping
- Painful urination
- Urinating more than once in a two hour period
- Increased urinating during hours of sleep

Risk factors: Female gender

Usual treatment:
- Behavior modification
- Medications (to reduce bladder contractions)
- Implantation of devices to strengthen pelvic muscles

• Surgery

Usual course: Varies depending upon the type; short- to long- term

Spiritual considerations:
• Despite the personal and sensitive nature of this condition, encourage the person to discuss concerns and feelings.
• Instill hope.
• Explore ways to engage the person in social activities.

Suggested scriptures: Psalms 73: 26; Philippians 4: 19

Resources:
National Institute of Aging
Building 31, Room 5C27
31 Center Drive, MSC 2292
Bethesda, MD 20892
800–222–2225

National Institute of Diabetes and Digestive and Kidney Disease
National Diabetics Information Clearinghouse
1 Information Way
Bethesda, MD 20892–3560
1–800–860–8747
www.niddk.nih.gov/health/urolog/urolog.htm

American Foundation for Urologic Disease
Bladder Health Council
800–242–2383
www.incontinence.org/index.html

SKIN AND BONE PROBLEMS

Arthritis (OA = Osteoarthritis; RA = Rheumatoid Arthritis)
Description: Joint disease that involves progressive loss of cartilage in the joints, leading to production of irregular bone deposits called

bone spurs. There are many types of arthritis; *OA* (also called *DJD:* degenerative joint disease) is the most common; *RA* is a chronic inflammatory arthritis involving the joints of the arms, legs, hands, and feet. *RA* can appear in much younger patients than *OA* and leads to severe deformities of the hands and fingers, resulting in disability

Incidence: *OA:* Very common (the majority of older people; sixty million people at any one time); *RA:* Less common (.3–1.5 percent of Americans)

Prevalence: *OA:* Males equally with females; over age sixty-five; *RA:* Females more than males overall; Native Americans (up to around five percent)

Signs and symptoms:
OA:
- Joint pain (comes on slowly; especially after movement)
- Stiffness (especially in the morning)
- Decreased range of motion

RA:
- Bone erosion
- Joint deformities
- Fatigue
- Depression
- (All symptoms listed above for OA)

Risk factors:
OA:
- Advanced age (over age fifty)
- Obesity
- Injury to a joint
- Stress over time to joints (sports- or job-related)

RA:
- Family history
- Female

- Ages twenty to fifty
- Native American background

Usual treatment:
- Medication (to reduce joint inflammation; in *RA*, to suppress the immune response)
- Lifestyle changes (proper weight maintenance, exercise, joint protection)
- Other therapies (heat, aquatic exercise)
- Surgery (such as joint replacement, for those who have significant pain or loss of function or mobility, especially in *RA*)

Usual course: Varies, but generally is progressive; poorer prognosis with *RA* because of chronic inflammation leading to loss of function. Neither *RA* nor *OA* is curable, so the goal of treatment is control. This means continuous treatment efforts. Severe forms of *RA* in young adults can render them totally disabled.

Spiritual considerations:
- Functional ability varies with severity and type of arthritis. Persons may become more disabled over time. Make sure your facility is accessible to affected individuals.
- Pain is a major factor. Provide comfort and reassurance. New medications are being developed.

Suggested scriptures: Isaiah 35: 3–4; Proverbs 17:22

Resources:
Arthritis Foundation
www.arthritis.org

Gout

Description: A defect in metabolism causes uric acid to build up in the blood leading to deposits in the joints that result in pain, swelling, and redness similar to arthritis; often occurs in the big toe, though any joints may be affected.

Incidence: 100 cases per 100,000 in the US; increases with age

Prevalence: Males much more than females

Signs and symptoms:
- Severe pain
- Swelling
- Redness (looking like an infection in the joint)
- Warmth
- Can flare up and then disappear

Risk factors:
- Family history
- Certain medications
- Obesity
- High blood pressure
- Diabetes
- Kidney problems
- Blood or skin disorders
- Polynesian descent
- Excessive use of alcohol

Usual treatment:
- Determination of the underlying cause
- Medication for the acute attack (to reduce inflammation and remove uric acid)
- Lifestyle changes (decrease fat in diet; decrease drinking alcohol; where possible, decrease medications that cause arthritis)

Usual course:
- Good prognosis and hope for full recovery if treated early; can have recurrent attacks that make treatment more challenging if the underlying cause of the buildup of uric acid is not addressed; frequency of attacks can be reduced by the use of medications that prevent the formation of uric acid—the

metabolic by-product that accumulates in the joints and causes gout.

Spiritual considerations:
- While not a life-threatening disorder, gout is painful and requires resting of the joint during flare-ups. Home visits may be necessary as the person may be unable to attend worship services.
- The cause for most older people is the medications they have been taking (diuretics, also known as "water pills" are a common cause). The doctor may be switching their medications around to prevent gout, and this may be upsetting both physically and emotionally to the older person. Provide comfort, reassurance, understanding, and prayer.

Suggested scriptures: Psalms 37: 23–24

Resources:
Arthritis Foundation
www.arthritis.org

Osteoporosis

Description: A generalized progressive loss of bone density that causes the bones to become weaker and more likely to fracture. Addressing risk factors (*especially early prevention*) is the best way to combat the disease (see list of risk factors below).

Incidence: Common (more than twenty-five million people affected; about forty percent of women and up to fifteen percent of men in the US)

Prevalence: Females more than males; more common with advanced age; more common in Anglo-Americans and Asian-Americans than African-Americans and Hispanics

Signs and symptoms:
- Backache
- Unexplained broken bones
- Becoming shorter in height

Risk factors:
- Loss of estrogen (after menopause)
- Not enough calcium or Vitamin D in diet
- Not enough exposure to sunlight
- Lack of exercise
- Smoking
- Drinking alcohol
- Drinking caffiene
- Certain medications
- Family history
- Hormone imbalance
- Thin, blonde, fair skinned
- European or Asian descent

Usual treatment:
- Prevention in childhood and adolescence
- Medications for pain or disability
- Medications to improve bone density
- Physical therapy and rehabilitation as needed
- Treatment of related fractures
- Prevent falls
- Hormone replacement therapy
- Proper diet

Usual course: Can be controlled or stabilized with proper treatment. Because of increased risk of complications related to fractures, elderly persons may have more disability and even earlier death. Individuals with a family history of severe osteoporosis are predisposed to a more severe course of the disease in which treatment is less effective. This form progresses to marked back deformity and often agonizing compression fractures of the vertebrae.

Spiritual considerations:

- Severe pain can be caused by multiple tiny fractures related to this disease, especially in older women. Prayer and comfort, as well as visits at home or in nursing homes, can be helpful.
- Start a prevention program in your community. Risk can be reduced by teaching pre-teens to include enough calcium in their diets while bones are forming.
- Persons with osteoporosis have a high risk for falls. Be sure your facility is as safe and accessible as possible.

Suggested scriptures: Psalms 55:22; Proverbs 17:22

Resources:
National Osteoporosis Foundation
1232 22nd St. N.W.
Washington, DC 20037– 1292
(202) 223–2226
www.nof.org

Psoriasis

Description: A common, chronic, recurrent, scaly rash of unknown cause that may involve only a small area of the body or may be widespread. The patches are well demarcated and thickened. Psoriasis often involves the scalp. In severe cases, inflammatory arthritis may be seen along with it.

Incidence: Common (1,000–2,000 per 100,000 people in the US)

Predominance: Males equally with females; especially seen in late teens/early twenties and age fifty-seven to sixty.

Signs and symptoms:
- Itchy skin
- Arthritis (in more severe cases)
- Dry, scaly patches on top of red skin
- Mostly seen on the scalp, knees, and elbows

Risk factors:
- Skin irritation
- Infection
- Stress
- Hormonal changes
- Drinking alcohol

Usual treatment:
- Medication (usually topical, but immunosuppressives used in some cases)
- Special baths and shampoos
- Other treatments for itchiness

Usual course
- Usually improves with proper treatment but can be more serious in certain persons; there is no cure, and the disease tends to be episodic and unpredictable; may recur in the winter with decreased exposure to sunlight; the earlier the age of onset, the more severe the disease.

Spiritual considerations:
- This condition is not contagious, but may look disturbing to others. Assure the person and congregational members that treatment usually helps.
- Provide comfort and calm presence during flare-ups when the person may feel fear and anxiety.

Suggested scriptures: Psalms 73:26; Job 19:26

Resources:
National Psoriasis Foundation
Suite 300, 6600 SW 92nd Avenue
Portland, OR 97223
1–800–723–9166

Warts

Description: Rough-surfaced, round or irregular firm nodules on the skin; usually less than one-half inch in diameter; caused by at least sixty different types of viruses. Warts can occur at any age, though are most common in children. They can be caught by skin-to-skin contact and may spread. Most are not painful, though plantar warts (often found on the soles of the feet) can be very painful.

Incidence: Common (up to ten percent of the US population)

Prevalence: Females more than males; more common in children and young adults

Signs and symptoms:
- Usually looks like a rough, raised, flesh-colored area of thick skin
- Often found on the hands and certain kinds on the feet

Risk factors:
- Skin trauma or infection
- Being in locker rooms frequently
- Skin to skin contact with someone having warts
- Impaired immune system

Usual treatment:
- Medication (topical agents that destroy the wart tissue)
- Freezing or cutting in the doctor's office
- Cover the warts during treatment to prevent spread

Usual course: May be variable; most are cured with treatment; some go away on their own over time; sometimes recur at the same site or different sites

Spiritual considerations:
- Warts are contagious, so educate your congregation about transmission and make appropriate policies for nursery work-

ers. If your facility includes a gym with locker rooms or showers, encourage people to use footwear in the locker room.
• Warts are highly curable, so offer hope. Warts on the feet can
  be painful and restrict mobility, so be sensitive to this possibility.

Suggested scriptures: 1 Peter 3:4

Resources:
American Association of Dermatology
www.aad.org/pamphlets/warts.html

Ear, Nose, and Throat Disorders
Otitis Media (Middle Ear Infection, also called Earache)
Description: Otitis media is a bacterial or viral infection in the middle ear that usually occurs after a cold or other upper respiratory
infection.

Incidence: Common; mostly in young children (three months to
three years)

Prevalence: Males

Signs and symptoms:
• Ear pain and/or pressure
• Temporary hearing loss
• Irritability
• Fever
• Tugging at ear(s)
• Fluid coming from ear

Risk factors:
• Frequent respiratory infections
• Male gender
• Exposure to childcare

- Exposure to tobacco smoke
- Bottle-fed
- Siblings with history of ear infections
- First infection before age four months

Usual treatment:
- Medication (antibiotics—take complete course of medication)
- Pain reliever
- Surgery (often needed to provide continuous drainage to the middle ear to prevent accumulation of fluid, also called "tubes in the ear")

Usual course: Usually clears up in a few days with appropriate antibiotic therapy, though hearing loss and permanent damage to the ear drum could result with continued or untreated infection.

Spiritual considerations: Support as needed

Suggested scriptures: Psalm 103: 2–3

Resources:
National Institute on Deafness and Other Communication Disorders
NIH
31 Center Drive, MSC 2320
Bethesda, MD 20892–2320
(301) 496–7243
www.nidcd.nih.gov/

Sinusitis
Description: An inflammation of the sinuses due to viral, bacterial, or fungal infections or allergic reactions. Sinuses are empty spaces within the facial bones. Each sinus is connected to the nose and surrounds the nose (termed "paranasal"). Germs gain entrance to the sinuses, usually during a cold or other viral infection, causing congestion and further blockage. This accumulation of fluid in the sinuses promotes growth of bacteria.

Incidence: Common (thirty-seven million Americans per year)

Prevalence: Males equally with females

Signs and symptoms:
- Headache
- Pain (forehead, upper jaw and teeth, between eyes, nose, ears, neck)
- Fever
- Weakness
- Fatigue
- Cough
- Nasal congestion
- Runny nose

Risk factors:
- Common cold
- Environmental exposure to allergens or pollutants
- Asthma
- Small growths in the nose

Usual treatment:
- Medication (appropriate antibiotics and medications to open sinus passages)
- Gentle heat to inflamed area
- Surgery (opening of the sinuses—in severe cases)

Usual course: Sinusitis can be cleared in a few days with appropriate treatment. Recurrent episodes may be common and can lead to a chronic condition; efforts to control allergic response are often needed.

Spiritual considerations: Instill hope for chronic cases of sinusitis

Suggested scriptures: 2 Corinthians 1:3–4

Resources:
National Institute of Allergy and Infectious Diseases
Office of Communications and Public Liaison
Building 31, Room 7A-50
31 Center Drive MSC 2520
Bethesda, MD 20892–2520
www.niad.nih.gov/factsheets/sinusitis.htm

Strep Throat (Streptococcal Pharyngitis)

Description: Infection of the throat caused by a bacterium called *streptococcus*, with acute onset. Twenty percent of persons with strep throat will have sore throat, fever, beefy red throat and white coating to the tonsils. The remainder of persons may have no symptoms except fever or mild sore throat, or have nonspecific symptoms such as headache, fatigue, nausea, vomiting, or fast heart beat. Cough, laryngitis, and stuffy nose are *not* usual symptoms.

Incidence: Common; especially among children ages six to twelve

Prevalence: Males equally with females

Signs and symptoms:
- Red and sore throat
- Enlarged lymph nodes in the neck
- White patches on tonsils
- Headache
- Fever
- Aches
- Upset stomach and vomiting

Risk factors:
- Age (children)
- Close social proximity (families, schools, childcare centers)

Usual treatment:
- Medication (antibiotics—usually for at least ten days)

- Acetaminophen (Tylenol®)

Usual course: Usually clears within days with appropriate treatment; left untreated, strep throat can result in serious injury to other organs later, such as the heart and kidneys.

Spiritual considerations: Support as needed

Suggested scriptures: Psalms 57:1

Resources:
National Institute of Allergy and Infectious Diseases
Office of Communications and Public Liaison
Building 31, Room 7A-50
31 Center Drive MSC 2520
Bethesda, MD 20892–2520

Tonsillitis

Description: Tonsillitis means infection of the tonsils—a condition most common in early childhood. The most common bacterium to infect the tonsils is streptococcus (see section on Strep Throat).

Incidence: Most common in children, because the tonsils are larger

Prevalence: Males equally with females

Signs and symptoms:
- Sore throat
- Difficulty swallowing
- Fever
- Headache
- Tiredness
- Soreness in glands in the neck

Risk factors:
- Age (children less than age seven)

- Exposure to groups
- Exposure to tobacco smoke

Usual treatment:
- Medication (antibiotics)
- Surgery (rare)

Usual course: Usually clears within a few days with antibiotic therapy. If the tonsils become repeatedly infected, they may need to be removed. On rare occasions, severe infections may lead to an abscess behind the tonsil, which may cause the throat to swell and jeopardize breathing. This situation is a medical emergency.

Spiritual considerations: Support as needed

Suggested scriptures: Psalms 5

Resources:
www.kidshealth.org/parent

BLOOD AND HORMONAL CONDITIONS
Diabetes
Description: Actually a group of diseases, diabetes is a condition in which the body is unable to properly metabolize glucose (or sugar). A person with diabetes has insufficient insulin (Type 1) or cells that do not respond to the insulin produced by the body, a condition that leads to an increase of glucose in the body (Type 2).

Diabetes is characterized by high blood sugar and is incurable. A person with diabetes must be treated for the rest of his or her life.

Incidence: Common (nearly sixteen million Americans; six percent of the US population)

Prevalence: Males equally with females (except gestational diabetes, which occurs only in females)

Signs and symptoms:
- High blood sugar (hyperglycemia)
- Increased frequency of urination
- Weight loss (though appetite remains)
- Increased thirst
- Blurred vision
- Fatigue
- Infections
- Diabetic coma (diabetic ketoacidosis-DKA)
- Nausea
- Vomiting
- Lethargy
- Fruity breath odor
- Increased respiration
- Dehydration
- Abdominal pain

Risk factors:
- Heredity
- Age (type 1: children; type 2: more than forty years of age)
- Race (type1: predominantly Anglo-Americans; type 2: predominantly African-Americans, Native Americans, and Hispanics)
- Obesity (in type 2)

Usual treatment:
Type 1
- Insulin
- Strict diet
- Regular eating patterns

Type 2
- Diet and weight loss
- Exercise
- Oral medication
- Insulin (one-third of all patients require insulin)

Usual course: Diabetes lasts a lifetime, but when it is adequately controlled with medications and diet, a person's life span need not be shortened. Uncontrolled diabetes can lead to serious and even fatal complications. Poor control of this disease results in the long-term complications of heart attack, stroke, kidney failure, blindness, and amputations. Short-term complications can include coma and death. People with diabetes have a poorer resistance to infection and are slower to heal.

Spiritual considerations:
- Encourage close adherence to prescribed treatment to reduce risk of complications.
- Be aware that medications taken for diabetes may cause sexual dysfunction.
- Use prayer and meditation to help reduce stress levels.
- Instill hope.

Suggested scriptures: Psalms 43:5; Philippians 4:4–7

Resources:
National Diabetics Information Clearinghouse
1 Information Way
Bethesda, MD 20892–3560
1–800–860–8747

American Diabetes Association
1701 North Beauregard Street
Alexandria, VA 22311
1–800–DIABETES
(1–800–342–2383)

Grave's Disease (Hyperthyroidism)
Description: Grave's disease, the most common form of hyperthyroidism in people under 40, is a condition in which the thyroid gland produces too much thyroid hormone. (Other, milder forms of

hyperthyroidism, can occur.) As a result, the body speeds up, pro-
ducing the classic symptoms of hyperthroidism.

Incidence: Common—two percent of all women in the US

Prevalence: Females

Signs and symptoms:
- Weight loss
- Muscle weakness
- Irritability
- Increased heart rate
- Nervousness
- Shaky hands
- Hair loss
- Protruding eyeballs
- Increased sweating
- Increased bowel movements
- Decreased menstrual flow

Risk factors:
- Female gender
- Heredity
- Age (twenty to forty years of age)

Usual treatment:
- Radioactive iodine medication
- Medication (antithyroid drugs)
- Surgery to remove thyroid gland

Usual course: Short (terminated by treatment)

Spiritual considerations:
- Encourage the person to explore feelings associated with this
  condition.

- Use of coping strategies such as prayer, meditation, and relaxation can help to decrease stress.

Suggested scriptures: Matthew 6:25–27

Resources:
Thyroid Society for Education and Research
7515 South Main St.
Suite 545
Houston, TX 77030
1–800–THY-ROID

Thyroid Foundation of America, Inc.
410 Stuart Street
Boston, MA 02116
800–832–8321
www.allthyroid.org/

*Human Immunodeficiency Virus/Acquired Immunodefiency
Virus (HIV/AIDs)*
Description: AIDS refers to the active disease caused by the HIV virus. It is important to know that you can have HIV without having AIDS. Requiring body fluid to body fluid contact for transmission, HIV/AIDS is a blood-borne virus. AIDS destroys the immune system at the cellular level, leaving the bodies of those infected weakened and susceptible to life-threatening infections.

Incidence: Not uncommon (nearly two million people infected in US; seventy million people infected worldwide)

Prevalence: Males (though the number of infected females is increasing)

Signs and symptoms:
- HIV

- Fatigue
- Swollen lymph glands
- Fever
- Night sweats
- Rapid weight loss
- Dry cough
- Diarrhea lasting more than one week
- White spots on tongue, mouth, throat
- Blotches (red, brown, pink, or purplish) on or under skin
- Pneumonia
- Memory loss
- Depression

Risk factors:
- Unprotected sex with person that is HIV positive
- Unprotected sex with multiple partners
- Sharing contaminated needles with IV drug use
- Received blood transfusion prior to 1985
- Newborn and nursing infants of HIV-positive mother

Usual treatment:
- Medication (antiretroviral drugs)
- Positive self-care

Usual course: Long-term with no cure

Spiritual considerations:
- Be sensitive to crisis points with this condition, including time of diagnosis, status change to AIDS, and approaching death
- Encourage open discussion of feelings and fears
- Promote support system
- Instill hope

Suggested scriptures: John 3:16; Colossians 3: 1–4; Revelation 21:1–4

Resources:
Center for Disease Control
National Center for HIV, STD, and TB Prevention
1108 Corporate Square
Atlanta, GA 30329
24/7 Hotline: 800–342–AIDS (2437)
Spanish Hotline: 800–344–SIDA (7432)
TTY Hotline: 800–243–7889
www.cdc.gov/nchstp/

Leukemia

Description: A group of cancers that affect the bone marrow and lymph system (blood-forming tissues) of the body. In this disease, abnormal white cells are produced that impair the body's ability to fight off infection.

Incidence: Rare (Two percent of all cancers; ten times more common in adults than children)

Prevalence: Males equally with females

Signs and symptoms:
• Fatigue
• Weakness
• Weight Loss
• Fever
• Bone or joint pain
• Swollen lymph nodes
• Decreased resistance to infections
• Bruising, bleeding (including nose bleeds)
• Abdominal fullness

Risk factors:
• Age (chronic after age sixty, acute forms affect children)
• Certain chemotherapy

- Environmental factors (radiation, paint removers containing benzene)
- Smoking
- High-dose radiation
- Toxins
- genetic susceptibility

Usual treatment:
- Chemotherapy
- Bone marrow transplant
- Interferon-alfa
- Stem-cell transplant
- Radiation
- Cell-specific antibodies

Usual course: Long-term, varies

Spiritual considerations:
- Instill hope.
- Allow the person to share feelings that may include shock, fear, sadness, guilt, hopelessness, and helplessness.
- Be attentive to suggestions of suicidal thoughts.
- Be aware that a diagnosis of cancer affects the entire family.

Suggested scriptures: Psalms 23; Psalms 27

Resources:
American Cancer Society (ACS)
1599 Clifton Rd., NE
Atlanta, GA 30329–4251
(800) 227–2345

National Cancer Institute
Cancer Information Service
Building 31, Room 10A03
31 Center Drive, MSC 2580

Bethesda, MD 20892–2580
800–4–CANCER (800–422–6237)
www.cis.nci.nih.gov/

Lymphoma

Description: This cancer affects the lymph tissues, the part of the body that is concerned with resisting infections. The two main types of lymphoma are Hodgkin's disease and non-Hodgkin's Lymphoma.

Incidence: Rare

Prevalence: Males

Signs and symptoms:
- Swollen lymph nodes
- Abdominal pain
- Itchy skin
- Fever
- Night sweats
- Fatigue
- Weight loss

Risk factors:
- Age (some more common in adults, others in children)
- Male gender
- Environmental factors (chemicals)
- Heredity
- Viral infections (Epstein-Barr virus, human immunodeficiency virus)

Usual treatment:
- Radiation
- Chemotherapy
- Bone marrow transplant
- Stem cell transplant

Usual course: Variable (Hodgkin's disease is considered the most curable form of blood cancer)

Spiritual considerations:
- A diagnosis of cancer affects the entire family.
- Allow the person to share feelings the may include shock, fear, sadness, guilt, hopelessness, and helplessness.
- Be attentive to suggestions of suicidal thoughts.
- Instill hope.

Suggested scriptures: John 14:1; Psalm 27:1

Resources:
American Cancer Society (ACS)
1599 Clifton Rd., NE
Atlanta, GA 30329–4251
(800) 227–2345

National Cancer Institute
Cancer Information Service
Building 31, Room 10A03
31 Center Drive, MSC 2580
Bethesda, MD 20892–2580
800–4–CANCER (800–422–6237)
www.cis.nci.nih.gov/

Sickle Cell Anemia

Description: Usually affecting African-Americans, this inherited disorder is caused by a defective form of hemoglobin. The red blood cells become crescent shaped and die early, leading to a chronic shortage of red blood cells. In addition, the abnormal cells may stack up, causing blockages that can result in pain and damage to vital organs.

Incidence: Rare (though among African-Americans, one in 500 births; 2.5 million Americans are asymptomatic carriers of the disease)

Prevalence: Males equally with females

Signs and symptoms:
- Pain and swelling of hands and feet
- Fatigue
- Yellowing of skin and eyes
- Eye problems
- Delayed growth
- At risk for infections
- Shortness of breath
- Pain
- Stroke

Risk factors: Genetic (people whose ancestors came from Africa, the Mediterranean basin, the Middle East, and India)

Usual treatment:
- Pain killing medications
- Blood transfusions

Usual course: Chronic (currently no cure)

Spiritual considerations:
- This disease affects the entire family.
- Parents may blame themselves for passing on this disease to their child, and are at risk for marital discord.
- Helplessness is often expressed because of the painful nature of this disease and the lack of a cure.

Suggested scriptures: Mark 10:13–16

Resources:
National Heart, Lung and Blood Institute
11 Rockledge Center
6701 Rockledge Drive, MSC 7950

Bethesda, MD 20892–7950
(301) 435–0055

Sickle Cell Disease Association of America
4221 Wilshire Blvd.
Los Angeles, CA 90010
1–800–421–8453

The Sickle Cell Information Center
P.O. Box 109
Grady Memorial Hospitcal
80 Jessie Hill Jr. Drive SE
Atlanta, GA 30303
www.emoryedu/PEDS/SICKLE

Other Medical Conditions

Cancer

Description: Cancer is really a group of diseases characterized by the growth of abnormal cells. As cancer cells accumulate, they form tumors. Not only can these tumors invade healthy tissues, they can also secrete enzymes or hormones that impair the body's function. *Metastasis* refers to the process by which cancer cells spread from the original site to other parts of the body.

Incidence: Common (nine million Americans)

Prevalence: Varies with type of cancer: females have a one in three lifetime risk of developing cancer (lung, breast, colon and rectum); males have a one in two lifetime risk of developing cancer (lung, prostate, colon and rectum, pancreas, stomach, liver)

Signs and symptoms:
- Varies with form of cancer, but may include:
- Lump or thickening in breast or other body part

- Unusual bleeding or discharge
- Change in bowel or bladder habits
- A sore throat that does not heal
- Nagging cough or hoarseness
- Indigestion or difficulty swallowing
- An obvious change in a mole or wart

Risk factors:
- Heredity
- Age
- Race
- Environmental factors:
- Smoking (especially lung, cancers of the mouth, pancreatic, bladder, cervical)
- Diet
- Infectious disease
- Chemicals
- Radiation

Usual treatment:
- Surgery
- Radiation
- Chemotherapy
- Hormonal therapy
- Immunotherapy

Usual course: Varies with the type and stage of cancer, the effectiveness of treatment, as well as patient's age and general health status

Spiritual considerations:
- Instill hope.
- Allow the person to share feelings that may include shock, fear, sadness, guilt, hopelessness, and helplessness.
- Be attentive to suggestions of suicidal thoughts.
- Be aware that a diagnosis of cancer affects the entire family.

Suggested scriptures: Psalms 31

Resources:
American Cancer Society (ACS)
1599 Clifton Rd., NE
Atlanta, GA 30329–4251
(800) 227–2345

National Cancer Institute
Cancer Information Service
Building 31, Room 10A03
31 Center Drive, MSC 2580
Bethesda, MD 20892–2580
800–4–CANCER (800–422–6237)
www.cis.nci.nih.gov/

Fibromyalgia

Description: A chronic condition characterized by fatigue and pain that is widely distributed throughout the soft tissue of the musculoskeletal system.

Incidence: Not uncommon (two percent of the US population; five million Americans)

Prevalence: Females (eighty percent)

Signs and symptoms:
- Fatigue
- Sleep disturbances
- Pain (with pressure)
- Headaches
- Elevated sensitivity to various stimuli
- Irritable bowel syndrome
- Decreased concentration
- Variable moods
- Dizziness

• Numbness and tingling of hands or feet

Risk factors:
• Gender (female)
• Age (20–60 years)
• Disturbed sleep patterns
• Heredity

Usual treatment:
• Medication
• Education
• Exercise
• Stress management
• Physical therapy
• Occupational therapy
• Alternative and complementary therapies

Usual course: Varies, though often chronic

Spiritual considerations:
• Debilitating nature of this condition may leave person feeling alienated from society and hopeless about the future.
• Engage in congregational activities to counter the desire to withdraw from others.
• Encourage the use of coping strategies like prayer, meditation, imagery, and relaxation.

Suggested scriptures: Psalms 39: 4, 14

Resources:
National Institute of Arthritis, Musculoskeletal, and Skin Diseases
Information Clearinghouse
National Institute of Health
1 AMS Circle
Bethesda, MD 20892–3675
(877) 22NIAMS

Influenza (commonly known as the Flu)

Description: An acute viral respiratory infection caused by influenza viruses classified as types A or B because of slight differences in their ability to cause infection and response to treatment and vaccination.

Incidence: Quite common; up to half a million new cases each year

Prevalence: Males equally with females; most common in school-age children and young adults; a cause of death in the elderly

Signs and symptoms:
- High fever
- Achiness
- Sore throat
- Cough
- Headache
- Chills
- Chest pain

Risk factors:
- Being close in proximity to others who have it
- Prior lung or breathing problems

Usual treatment:
- Medication (antiviral drugs for prevention of type A)
- Rest
- Drink plenty of fluids
- Avoid smoking
- Use a humidifier for moisture in the air

Usual course: The disease can be quite severe, usually beginning forty-eight hours after exposure. Complete recovery occurs in most people, but the elderly are at higher risk for complications and death. Weakness and fatigue may persist for several days or occasionally for weeks. The occurrence of pneumonia is quite high during the course of this disease and may be life-threatening.

Spiritual considerations:
- Immunizations (flu vaccine) is generally recommended for those over age sixty-five. Faith communities may act as sites for flu shots by inviting the local health department to use your facility for vaccinations.
- Older adults may experience more severe symptoms and therefore require a longer period of support.

Suggested scriptures: Psalms 126: 5–6; Psalms 124: 8

Resources: www.cdc.gov/ncidod/disease/flu/fluvirus.htm

Insomnia

Description: This condition includes difficulty going to sleep, staying asleep or returning to sleep when awakened early.

Incidence: Common (one in three; seventy million Americans)

Prevalence: Common in both males and females, though insomnia affects more females

Signs and symptoms:
- Difficulty falling asleep
- Waking up through the night with difficulty returning to sleep.
- Early morning awakening
- Chronic fatigue

Risk factors:
- Increased age
- Female gender
- History of depression
- Stress and anxiety
- Underlying health conditions

Usual treatment:
- Treatment of underlying health conditions
- Behavior modification
- Medication
- Relaxation Therapy
- Sleep reconditioning

Usual course: Varies

Spiritual considerations:
- As a consequence of the fatigue, the person's work and relationships may suffer.
- Promote coping strategies such as prayer, meditation, and relaxation.

Suggested scriptures: Psalms 4:8

Resources:
National Center on Sleep Disorders Research
National Institutes of Health
Two Rockledge Centre
Suite 10038
6701 Rockledge Drive, MSC 7920
Bethesda, MD 20892–792
(301) 435–0199

Sudden Infant Death Syndrome (SIDS, also called Crib Death)
Description: Death of an infant under one year of age, for which there is no apparent explanation. Usually occurs when the baby is sleeping in crib.

Incidence: Rare (5,000 per year in US; usually less than four months of age)

Prevalence: Males

Signs and symptoms: Death

Risk factors:
- Race (African-Americans two to three times more than Anglo-Americans; Native Americans three times more than Anglo-Americans)
- Babies who sleep on stomachs
- Mother who smoked during pregnancy
- Environmental toxins, especially smoke
- Mother less than twenty-years-old with first pregnancy
- Limited or no prenatal care
- Low-birth-weight babies
- Premature babies
- Death of sibling to SIDS

Usual treatment: Reduce risk factors where possible, especially placing baby on its back to sleep

Usual course: N/A

Spiritual considerations:
- Such a tragic event in the life of any parent may lead to blaming behavior and questioning the presence of God.
- Remember that death affects the entire family, including other children.
- Long-term spiritual support may be indicated.
- The grief response may progress into major depression.

Suggested scriptures: 2 Corinthians 1: 3–4; John 11:25

Resources:
National Institute of Child Health and Human Development
Building 31, Room 2A32, MSC 2425
31 Center Drive
Bethesda MS 20892–2425

800–370–2943
www.nichd.nih.gov/publications/pubs/sidsfact.htm

Systemic Lupus Erythematosus (SLE)

Description: SLE is a chronic disorder of the immune system that may affect organs throughout the body. In this disease, the body develops antibodies that assault healthy tissues—especially the lungs, heart, kidneys, brain, skin and joints.

Incidence: Not uncommon (two million Americans)

Prevalence: Females

Signs and symptoms:
- Achy joints
- Arthritis
- Fatigue
- Fever (more than 100° F)
- Skin rashes
- Anemia
- Kidney damage
- Pain in the chest on deep breathing
- Rash on face
- Light or sun sensitivity
- Hair loss
- Raynaud's phenomenon
- Seizures
- Mouth or nose ulcers

Risk factors:
- Female gender
- Heredity
- Environmental factors

Usual treatment:
- Rest
- Stress management
- Avoid direct sunlight
- Balanced diet
- Medications
- Psychotherapy and family therapy
- Self-help group

Usual course: Long-term (mild to severe)

Spiritual considerations:
- SLE affects the entire family.
- Reactions of loss and grief frequently occur when the person is finally diagnosed.
- Instill hope.

Suggested scriptures: Psalms 3; Lamentations 3: 22–26

Resources:
The SLE. Foundation Inc.
149 Madison Avenue
Suite 205
New York, NY 10016
(212) 685–4118

Lupus Foundation of America, Inc.
1300 Piccard Drive
Suite 200
Rockville, MD 20850–4303
800–558–0121

EMOTIONAL, PSYCHOLOGICAL, AND SPIRITUAL CONCERNS

Anxiety Disorders (Panic Disorder, Post-Traumatic Stress Disorder, Obsessive-Compulsive Disorder, Generalized Anxiety Disorder, Phobias)

Description: A group of conditions associated with feelings of uncertainty, helplessness, diffuse apprehension, and of being threatened.

Incidence: Common (one in four; twenty-three million Americans; ten to twenty-five percent of the population)

Prevalence: Occurs in males and females in equal numbers

Signs and symptoms:
- Racing heart
- Change in blood pressure
- Faintness
- Rapid breathing and shortness of breath
- Loss of appetite
- Fidgeting
- Tremors
- Insomnia
- Interpersonal withdrawal
- Rapid speech
- Startle reaction
- Impaired thinking
- Fear
- Confusion

Risk factors:
- Heredity
- Fearful experiences
- Stress/threats
- Fatigue
- Illness

Usual treatment:
- Medication
- Cognitive-behavioral therapy

Usual course: Varies

Spiritual considerations:
- Foster feelings of safety and security.
- Use of prayer and meditation to reduce sense of helplessness and stress levels.
- Remain present and calm with the individual during acute episodes of anxiety.

Suggested scriptures: Philippians 4:6– 8; 2 Timothy 1:7

Resources:
National Alliance for the Mentally Ill (NAMI)
Colonial Place Three
2109 Wilson Blvd., Suite 300
Arlington, VA 22201–3042
Helpline: 1–800–950–6264 (NAMI)
www.nami.org/

Attention Deficit Hyperactivity Disorder (ADHD)
Description: A group of chronic conditions that begin in childhood and may continue throughout adult life. Commonly, those with ADHD have difficulty being still, paying attention, concentrating, and controlling their behavior.

Incidence: Relatively common (two million American children; three to five percent of children)

Prevalence: Males (two to three times greater than females)

Signs and symptoms:
- Inattention
- Carelessness
- Does not listen
- Unable to sit still
- Fidgets
- Distractible
- Impulsive
- Talks excessively
- Interrupts others
- Learning disabilities
- Anxiety and depression

Risk Factors:
- Heredity
- Maternal exposure to toxins, including smoking and drug use

Usual Treatment:
- Psychotherapy
- Behavior therapy
- Family therapy
- Medication
- Support group
- Parenting skills training

Usual course: Long-term, indefinite

Spiritual considerations:
- Provide parents opportunities to discuss feelings such as self-doubt, blame, and guilt in a nonjudgmental manner.
- ADHD affects the entire family.
- Children enrolled in the congregation's educational programs may require additional supervision.

Suggested scriptures: Philippians 4:13; 1 Timothy 4:12; 2 Timothy 2:15

Resources:
Attention Deficit Information Network
475 Hillside Drive
Needham, MA 02494–1278
(781) 455–9895

Autism

Description: Usually appearing in the first three years of a child's life, autism is a brain disorder that causes a broad range of developmental disabilities. This disorder affects the child's behavior, social skills, and language skills.

Incidence: Not uncommon (about 500,000 Americans)

Prevalence: Males (four times more likely than females)

Signs and symptoms:
- Prefers to be alone
- Less responsive to social cues
- May experience hypersensitivity to sensory stimuli
- Limited to no use of speech
- Lack of spontaneous play
- Overactivity or passivity
- Tantrums
- Difficulty with changes in routine
- Performs repetitive movements
- Self-injury
- Rituals
- Preoccupation with parts of objects

Risk factors
Genetics/Heredity

Usual treatment:
- Medication

- Educational behavior therapy
- Social skills training

Usual course: A chronic condition with no cure

Spiritual considerations:
- Depending on the level of the child's disability, parents may feel exhausted, overwhelmed, and hopeless.
- Provide the family with nonjudgmental support (parents, especially mothers, were blamed for causing autism in the past).
- Parents may worry about what will happen to their child if they should die or become incapacitated (when the child has become an adult).

Suggested scriptures: Psalms 139: 1–4; Jeremiah 29:11

Resources:
Autism Society of America
National Institute of Neurological Disorders and Strokes (NINDS)
7910 Woodmont Avenue
Suite 300 P.O. Box 5801
Bethesda, MD 20814–3067 Bethesda, MD 20824
800–3AUTISM 800–352–9424
www.autism-society.org www.nihds.nih.gov

Bipolar Disorder (Manic Depressive Illness)
Description: Bipolar disorder is a psychological condition that affects mood, feelings, behavior, and physical health. It is characterized by dramatic mood swings from overly "high" to sad and hopeless.

Incidence: Uncommon (.6 percent to .88 percent of population; two million Americans)

Prevalence: Females

Signs and symptoms:
- Elevated, expansive or overly good mood
- Irritability
- Inflated self-esteem
- Racing thoughts
- Sleep disturbances, little sleep
- Inadequate nutrition and weight loss
- Poor judgment
- Distractible
- Impaired thinking
- Aggressiveness
- Hyperactivity and increased motor activity
- Excess of all kinds: spending, activity, verbosity, drugs
- Rapid, pressured speech

Risk factors:
- Heredity
- Stress
- Personality
- Female gender
- Family history of bipolar disorder

Usual treatment:
- Medication
- Psychoeducation
- Cognitive behavior therapy

Usual course: Often a chronic condition

Spiritual considerations:
- Severe and persistent nature of this illness affects every aspect of the person's life.
- Encourage the person to take medication as prescribed.
- Instill hope.
- See section on Depression.

Suggested scriptures: 2 Timothy 1:7

Resources:
National Alliance for the Mentally Ill (NAMI)
Colonial Place Three
2107 Wilson Blvd., Suite 300
Arlington, VA 22201–3042
800–950–NAMI (6264)

National Mental Health Association (NMHA)
1021 Prince Street
Alexandria, VA 22314–2971
800–969–NMHA

National Institute of Mental Health (NIMH)
Information Resources and Inquiries Branch
RM 7C-02, MSC 8030
Bethesda, MD 20892–8030
800–421–4211
www.nimh.nih.gov

Chemical Dependency and Drug Addiction

Description: The continued use of drugs or alcohol, including pre-scription medications, despite negative consequences—emotional, physical, social, and spiritual. May involve physical and emotional dependence as well as a negative experience if drug or alcohol is withdrawn.

Incidence: Common (14.8 million Americans use illicit drugs; 8.2 million Americans are chemically dependent or use alcohol)

Prevalence: Occurs in males and females in equal numbers

Signs and symptoms:
• Craving drugs or alcohol daily
• Overwhelmed by life situations

- Unable to stop drug or alcohol use
- Answer "yes" to two or more questions in CAGE self assessment tool (see page 206)

Risk factors:
- Heredity
- Depression
- Learning experiences
- Stress
- Peer pressure
- Poor academic achievement
- Chaotic home environment
- Poor social coping skills

Usual treatment:
- Detoxification (elimination of chemical[s] in the body's system)
- Counseling
- Behavioral medication
- Self-help group (AA)
- Medications

Usual course: Varies

Spiritual considerations:
- Denial that a problem exists is extremely common.
- Relapses are to be expected
- Addiction affects the entire family.
- Instill hope that through belief in God, the person has the power to overcome addiction.

Suggested scriptures: 2 Corinthians 4:6–11; 2 Corinthians 4: 16–18

Resources:
National Institute on Alcohol Abuse and Alcoholism
6000 Executive Blvd.

Wellco Building
Bethesda, MD 20892–7003

Depression

Description: Depression is a psychological condition that affects your mood, feelings, behavior, and physical health. It is characterized by chronic sadness.

Incidence: Common (one of 8; seven to twelve percent of men and twenty to thirty percent of women in America; 11.5 million cases per year)

Prevalence: Females

Signs and symptoms:
- Loss of interest or pleasure in everyday activities
- Ongoing sadness
- Sleep problems
- Impaired thinking or concentration
- Significant weight loss or gain
- Irritation or slowing of body movements
- Tiredness
- Focus on aches and pains
- Loss of interest in sex.
- Negative view of the future; hopelessness
- Thoughts of death or suicide
- Frequent crying

Risk factors:
- Heredity
- All ages and races
- Old age
- Lack of social support
- Divorced or single
- Women (hormonal changes, problems with neurotransmitters)
- Stressful life events

- Personal history of sexual abuse
- Substance abuse

Usual treatment:
- Medication
- Psychotherapy, especially cognitive therapy
- Light therapy
- Electroconvulsive therapy (ECT)
- Complementary alternative medication

Usual course: Varies, can be chronic

Spiritual considerations:
- There is an increased risk of suicide (and homicide).
- Depression can be confused with reactions of grief.
- Address feelings of helplessness and hopelessness.
- The person may consider him or herself unworthy of attention from the congregational staff member who gives it.

Suggested scriptures: Romans 8:28; Colossians 3: 15

Resources:
National Alliance for the Mentally Ill (NAMI)
Colonial Place Three
2107 Wilson Blvd., Suite 300
Arlington, VA 22201–3042
800–950–NAMI (6264)

National Mental Health Association (NMHA)
1021 Prince Street
Alexandria, VA 22314–2971
800–969–NMHA

Resources and Inquiries Branch
National Institute of Mental Health (NIMH)
Information RM 7C-02, MSC 8030

Bethesda, MD 20892–8030
800–421–4211
www.nimh.nih.gov

Eating Disorders

Description: A group of conditions characterized by disturbances in eating behavior that may include frequent overeating (binging), fasting, severe dieting, self-induced vomiting, laxative and diuretic use, and excessive exercise. Those affected are obsessively concerned with body weight.

Incidence: Fairly common (one to four percent of the American population; up to fifteen percent of high school girls in US, five million Americans)

Prevalence: Females

Signs and symptoms:
- Anorexia or bulimia
- Significant weight loss
- Extreme concern about weight
- Denial of hunger, body weight and image
- Missing periods
- Eating large amounts of food
- Sensitivity about body weight
- Excessive exercise
- Sneaking food
- Trips to the bathroom after meals
- Vomiting to purge food
- Use of laxatives
- Excessive exercise
- Loss of enamel on teeth
- Altered eating habits

Risk factors:
- Age (increases at puberty)

- Female gender
- Family dynamics
- Heredity
- Emotional disorders
- Extreme exercise programs

Usual treatment:
- Hospitalization may be required
- Psychotherapy
- Family therapy
- Educational groups
- Medication (antidepressants)

Usual course: Varies, though often long-term

Spiritual considerations:
- Personal and family denial of the condition is common.
- Issues of control and powerlessness are often central.
- Eating disorders can be life-threatening (a five percent mortality rate is associated with anorexia nervosa)
- The long-term nature of eating disorders may require sustained spiritual and emotional support.

Suggested scriptures: 1 Corinthians 6: 19–20; 1 Samuel 16: 7

Resources:
Resources and Inquiries Branch
National Institute of Mental Health (NIMH)
Information RM 7C-02, MSC 8030
Bethesda, MD 20892–8030
800–421–4211

Harvard Eating Disorders Center
356 Boylston Street
Boston, MA 02116
(617) 236–7766
www.hedc.org/

Obsessive-Compulsive Disorder (OCD)

Description: A condition characterized by anxious thoughts and/or rituals that the person believes he or she cannot control.

Incidence: Not common (one in fifty Americans; two percent of the population)

Prevalence: Males equally with females

Signs and symptoms:
- Unwanted ideas or impulses
- Repetitive behaviors (compulsion)
- Anxiety
- Frequent recognition of the unrealistic nature of a thought
- Fear of harm
- Fear of contamination
- Need to do things correctly
- Thoughts of violence
- Thoughts of sex

Risk factors:
- Heredity

Usual treatment:
- Medication
- Behavioral therapy

Usual course: Long-term

Spiritual considerations:
- Instill hope.
- The person's rituals can disrupt family routine.

- Use prayer and spiritual connectedness as a means to confront the person's sense of powerlessness.

Suggested scriptures: Colossians 3: 1–4; Philippians 4: 19

Resources:
Anxiety Disorders Association of America
11900 Parklawn Drive, Suite 100
Rockville, MD 20852, USA
(301) 231–9350

Resources and Inquiries Branch
National Institute of Mental Health (NIMH)
Information RM 7C-02, MSC 8030
Bethesda, MD 20892–8030
800–421–4211
www.nimh.nih.gov

Screening test for OCD
or
www.adaa.org/aboutanxietydisorders/ocd/ocdselftest

Post-Traumatic Stress Disorder (PTSD)

Description: PTSD follows a traumatic event in which a person feels actual or threatened harm to him- or herself. The person reexperiences the feelings of fear, helplessness, or horror, and avoids reminders associated with the trauma.

Incidence: Common (one to three percent of the US population has a severe form; five to fifteen percent of the population has a milder form)

Prevalence: Males equally with females

Signs and symptoms:
- Re-experiencing events through flashbacks or memories

- Emotional numbness
- Crying
- Increased use of drugs or alcohol
- Sleep disturbances
- Nightmares
- Frequently feeling overwhelmed by everyday situations
- Mood swings
- Irritability
- Feeling suspicious
- Feeling fearful
- Feeling guilty
- Having a sense of impending doom
- Withdrawal from others

Risk factors: Exposure to a life-threatening event that caused intense fear, helplessness or horror

Usual treatment:
- Medication
- Behavioral therapy
- Cognitive behavioral therapy

Usual course: Short- to long-term

Spiritual considerations:
- Offer encouragement to remain in treatment (there is a seventy percent treatment drop-out rate).
- Promote spiritual understanding of life events to move the person beyond the unanswerable question, "Why did this happen to me?"
- Use of prayer and meditation as coping strategies.

Suggested scriptures: Isaiah 26: 3–4; Psalms 91

Resources:
Anxiety Disorders Association of America
11900 Parklawn Drive, Suite 100
Rockville, MD 20852, USA
(301) 231–9350

Schizophrenia

Description: Schizophrenia is often a chronic and severe mental illness that affects the function of the brain. This disabling brain disease usually involves periods of psychosis, hallucinations and delusions, and alterations in behaviors.

Incidence: Not common (one percent of the US population, 2.7 million Americans)

Prevalence: Males equally with females

Signs and symptoms:
- Hallucinations (false sensory information, especially hearing voices)
- Delusions (false fixed personal beliefs)
- Emotionally-dulled responses
- Inappropriate emotions
- Bizarre behavior
- Disorganized speech
- Withdrawal
- Impaired relationships

Risk factors: Heredity, including neurological abnormalities of the brain

Usual treatment:
Medication
Rehabilitation
Psychotherapy
Education of the family
Support groups

Usual course: Usually chronic

Spiritual considerations:
- This condition affects the entire family.
- A support network may not exist because of the severe nature of this condition and the repeated strain on relationships.
- The person and family may feel hopeless and helpless against this disease.
- Encourage the person to remain in treatment.

Suggested scriptures: Psalms 138: 8; Psalms 40: 17

Resources:
National Institute of Mental Health (NIMH)
Information Resources and Inquiries Branch
RM 7C-02, MSC 8030
Bethesda, MD 20892–8030
800–421–4211
www.nimh.nih.gov

National Alliance for the Mentally Ill (NAMI)
Colonial Place Three
2107 Wilson Blvd., Suite 300
Arlington, VA 22201–3042
800–950–NAMI (6264)

PART TWO
STARTING AND DEVELOPING YOUR PROGRAM

FIVE

STARTING YOUR OWN
HEALTH PROGRAM

B ecause a health ministry requires wholehearted commitment, ownership, and participation, the congregation must be as clear as possible about its level of motivation from the start. This chapter begins with an inquiry into your congregation's motivation to start a health program and its understanding of a health ministry.

MOTIVATION AND GOALS

Worldwide, communities of faith consider the health of the individual and the collective congregation as a component of their higher mission. For Christians, the centrality of health and healing is evident in Biblical teachings and in current congregational practices. Tending to the mind, body, and spirit of the parishioners is embedded in a rich history of compassionate caring within congregations.

Still, it is important to understand why your congregation chooses to devote time, space, and money to a health ministry when the same resources could be used for daycare programming, evangelism, youth groups, social ministry, or senior activities—to name a few. To be sure, many congregations serve all of these functions and more, but most must be very deliberate in the way they use their resources.

Here are some of the questions you must consider before you come to the decision to take on the tasks of a health ministry:

- Is the request for the health ministry program coming from many members of your congregation or only a few?
- Is there a broad demand for programming from all age groups or only from one group?
- Are these requests for health education programs, health screenings, and health promotion, or do people want actual delivery of care?
- Are there members of the congregation qualified to organize and oversee such programs?
- Are these people interested in serving in the health ministry programs?
- How supportive of a health ministry are the members of the congregation's professional staff?
- Do the lay leaders of the church support this idea?

Answering these questions is essential to clarifying the vision of the congregational health ministry. In some cases, the answers may tell you that you are not ready yet, and they may help you to define the jobs needed to get you ready.

Assuming that you find that you *are* ready, you must clarify the health-related goals of the congregation. For example, if many members of your congregation are uninsured or underinsured and do not have their own health care providers, your goals probably would include the active treatment of illness. If most of your members *do* have adequate insurance and health care already, your ministry may want to concentrate on improving overall health and promoting positive lifestyle changes of the members.

But whatever the specific needs of your program, we can say that most health ministries focus on the following goals:

- Improving overall health through health education and health promotion activities.
- Preventing potential disease through risk appraisals, screening programs, and disease prevention activities.
- Diagnosing and treating new cases of illness.

- Maintaining an optimal level of health with known illnesses or conditions.

Your program may have a single emphasis or be multipurpose. There is no one way to have a successful program, but all successful programs begin with a clear vision and established goals.

DETAILS, DETAILS, DETAILS

With an identified vision and set goals, you move into the practical issues of creating a health ministry program. What organizational structure will your program use? To answer that, you may need a little history.

The movement toward pairing the traditional health care community with the faith community began in the late 1960s with the work of Rev. Granger Westberg. These early efforts have crystallized today into *parish or congregational nursing.*

We encourage you to read *Parish Nursing: Promoting Whole Person Health within Faith Communities.* (See this citation at the end of Chapter 1.) We also refer you back to Chapter 1 for an account of the role the parish nurse can play in your program.

As you consider the organizational structure of your program, you will need to address additional questions. While your list will certainly be even longer, here are some of those questions:

- Who will be responsible for your health program? What qualifications do you require?
- To whom will your health coordinator report?
- Will the health coordinator be paid or unpaid? If paid, how will you raise these dollars?
- Will you collaborate with other congregations? Or agencies?
- What resources will you need—including space, equipment, personnel, and materials?
- How will you train volunteers?
- Have you considered liability insurance?
- Where will you refer persons who need more care than you can provide?

- What documentation system will you use?
- How will physicians and other health care providers be involved?

How you answer these questions will be critical to the success of your program. Remember that this is a project of faith and grit!

In this chapter, we have asked more questions than we have provided answers. This is appropriate since no one but you can set up your health ministry program. The point we want to make is that your congregation must be fully engaged in the program. In order to be fully engaged, each member needs to feel responsible for his or her own health (or illness).

Such responsibility will take some learning and change, since it departs from the way health care is generally practiced today in the United States. A health ministry model places the person at the center and attends to his or her physical, emotional, social and spiritual well-being. *Through the health ministry program, members of the congregation will be empowered to take charge of their own health.*

SIX

HANDLING COMMON EMERGENCIES

Within the church setting, you will sometimes need to know basic first aid. Accidents may happen in the nursery, such as bumps and bruises, cuts and scrapes, and sometimes more serious situations. Adolescents and adults may also experience accidents or sudden health problems that require quick and knowledgeable attention. This chapter will give you some basic first aid tips.

Remember that if you are unsure of what do to in an emergency, it is better to err on the side of caution. That is, if you don't know how badly a person is hurt, get medical help.

FIRST AID FOR COMMON EMERGENCIES

Bites

Human bites, such as toddlers give and receive in the play room, can usually be treated by washing with soap and warm water. Be sure to tell the injured child's parents exactly what happened. Teach children that biting hurts others. Never show a child that biting hurts by biting them back or allowing others to do the same, because such reaction just sets a bad example and does not help improve anyone's behavior.

If a person has been bitten by an animal, wash the area with soap and water and then carefully look at the wound. If there is a lot of bleeding or the area is deeply punctured or gaping, the person should see a doctor. In the meantime, cover the area with a clean cloth or bandage.

If the person has been bitten by a snake or a spider, write down a description of the animal and call your local Poison Control Center for further instructions. Keep the person still and calm. If the bite is on an arm or leg, keep the limb slightly below the level of the heart. In areas where poisonous snakes or spiders are common, be sure to have a plan in place in case of an emergency. If the snake was killed, keep its head for identification.

Broken Bones

If someone has fallen and you can see obvious deformity of the injured part, treat it as a broken bone. The injured person may not want you to touch the injured part. If the injured person is a child, he or she may not stop crying.

- Sometimes if a bone is broken, the area will get swollen and discolored. Other times there will not be many outward signs, but the person will have pain and find it difficult to use the injured part.
- If a person has a neck or back injury, treat it as an emergency and call an ambulance. Do not move the person.
- If you suspect a broken leg or arm, do not move it until it has been splinted.

In all cases but the obviously minor ones, have the person seek medical help.

Bruises

If a bruise is small, an ice pack or cool cloth should be applied for about fifteen minutes, which will decrease swelling and pain. With children, if the bruise is large, swollen, or very painful, notify the parents so they can decide how to treat the injury. *Bruises indicate tissue damage and bleeding, and adults with large bruises may also need medical attention if other injury has been sustained.* For all bruises, whether in children or adults, note how the injury occurred. Observe whether the bruised area was bumped, pinched or crushed.

Burns

Remember the words: STOP, DROP, and ROLL. Reinforce this teaching to the children in your church about what to do if their clothes catch on fire.

- For small burns that leave only a red spot, place the burned area in cool water for fifteen minutes.
- If the area burned is large or severe, the person will need medical treatment. Call an ambulance.
- Do not break blisters from a burn.
- Do not use ice directly on the area, as this can damage the skin further.
- Vaseline, oils, or butter should not be put on a burn because they can seal in the heat and make it worse.

Have a doctor evaluate more serious burns.

Choking

If a person is unable to breathe, cough, or talk from choking on food or an object, call an ambulance. Encourage coughing. Strong coughing can often dislodge the material causing the trouble.

If the person choking is conscious and he or she is holding a hand to his or her throat (the universal distress sign for choking), you may be able to help by using *the Heimlich maneuver. To do the Heimlich maneuver* from behind the person, put both of your arms around his or her waist. Make a fist with one hand and tuck your thumb in. Place that hand just above the person's belly button, but below the ribs, with the thumb side of your fist pressing into the tummy. Place your other hand on top of that hand. Press the hands in and upward with moderate force to try to expel the object choking the person. You are pushing underneath the diaphragm when doing the Heimlich maneuver and it will look like you are giving the person a forceful hug from the back. Continue until the object comes out or the person becomes unconscious. (Members of the congregation may want to practice the Heimlich maneuver on one another.)

If the person choking becomes unconscious, stay with him or

her until help arrives. If you are trained in CPR (cardiopulmonary resuscitation), use those skills to help the unconscious person.

Cuts

Most cuts that people sustain in the church setting will be minor and can be handled by church lay people. However, cuts *can* be serious, particularly if they happen while people are using dangerous tools such as they might be, for example, while working on renovations to the building.

If a cut is spurting blood, an artery may have been damaged and the person may lose a lot of blood. Call an ambulance.

For any other type of bleeding, the treatment is basically the same. Place a clean cloth or clean paper towels or clothing over the wound. Apply firm pressure with your hand. *Applying firm pressure is the best immediate way to stop bleeding.*

In serious cases, do not stop applying pressure until help arrives. In cases of minor injury, it may be enough to wash the area with soap and water and apply a bandage or other nonstick dressing. *Keep these supplies in your house of worship's emergency first aid kit.*

Fainting

There are many reasons why a person might faint—that is, pass out. Common causes in our faith community settings might include:

- exposure to very hot weather
- not eating or drinking for a long period of time
- standing too long in one place with one's knees locked (such as might occur during a church program)
- side-effects from medication

Older people sometimes feel dizzy or faint when they get up quickly, because their blood pressure drops suddenly.

If a person tells you he or she feels faint, have him or her lie down with the legs raised. You can help elevate the legs, being sure to protect a woman's privacy as necessary if she is wearing a dress or skirt. To raise the legs you may want to place them on a pillow or on a chair. The idea is to have the legs above the level of the chest (or the heart) to promote better blood flow to the brain.

Do not give a person who has fainted anything to eat or drink. If the person does not wake up right away, call for emergency assistance.

Consider having smelling salts available to help rouse a person who has fainted.

Head or Neck Injuries

These types of injuries usually happen as the result of accidents or falls. In the church setting, this could include car accidents in the parking lot or on trips, falls from ladders or platforms, or trauma from sports activities.

- Do not move a person who may have suffered a serious head, neck, or back injury. You could make the injury worse.
- If there is loss of consciousness, seizures, dizziness, headache, complaints of feeling sick, or blood coming from the eyes, ears, or nose, call an ambulance. In the meantime, keep the person warm and stay with him or her until help arrives.

Nosebleeds

Most nosebleeds can be handled by church staff. Causes of nose-bleeds may include:
- injury (getting bumped or hit in the face or nose)
- excessive dryness
- other unexplained reasons

Among small children, nosebleeds most often occur from nose picking or from injury.

To treat a nosebleed:
- Have the person sit down
- Have the person lean forward(do not tip the head far back-wards or have him or her lie down, because this makes blood drip down the throat)
- Squeeze the outside of the nostrils firmly right below the bridge of the nose between your thumb and first finger *steadily*

for about ten minutes. Some people tend to bleed more than others (or their blood clots more slowly), so you may need to hold the nose longer.

A person should not blow his or her nose during or right after a nosebleed, because this act can worsen the condition. The person should sit quietly until the bleeding stops.

Most nosebleeds are minor and will stop with this treatment. If the bleeding is very heavy, or continues for a long period of time, the person will need to see a doctor.

Poisoning

Prevention is always best, especially when it comes to poisons. Many poisonings occur among children each year—and most are preventable. Poisonous substances can be anything from medications to cleaning supplies.

- Make sure that all cleaning fluids, medications, or other potentially dangerous substances are well out of the reach of children and/or in a locked cupboard or closet.
- Place stickers with "icky" faces on containers to remind people, especially children, that this is not a substance to eat or drink.

If a child or other person has eaten or drunk something that might be hurtful, call your local Poison Control Center immediately for instructions. The phone number for Poison Control should be handy near telephones throughout your facility and should also be on a sheet of emergency numbers in your first aid kit.

The trained people at Poison Control will ask you questions. Be sure to have handy the bottle or container the substance was in so that you can describe it to them over the phone. They will give you specific instructions as to what to do. A web site at www.parentsplace.com/health/firstaid gives a list of Poison Control Centers and phone numbers.

If, after taking the substance, the person has trouble breathing, has seizures, becomes unconscious, or shows abnormal symptoms or behavior, call an ambulance.

Ipecac Syrup should be included in all church emergency kits for the purpose of causing the person to vomit if that is the Poison Control Center's prescribed treatment. Not all poisonings can be treated in this way, however. Some poisons (such as gasoline or other very toxic liquids) would burn the throat if the person were made to vomit them up.

Most poisonings will require a trip to the emergency room for evaluation and treatment. Always take the bottle containing the poison with you to the emergency room.

Puncture Wounds

If the puncture wound is minor, from, for example, stepping on a tack, remove the object and cleanse the wound with soap and water. If the object is large (such as a stick, knife, or piece of metal), do not try to remove it yourself. Seek emergency medical help.

Most puncture wounds are minor and can be handled by your staff. However, if the person has stepped on a rusty object such as a nail, he or she will need to be sure that his or her tetanus shot is current. *Puncture wounds sometimes cause tetanus, a serious illness that sometimes can result in severe muscle spasms and even death if untreated.*

Always notify the parents if a child has suffered a puncture wound.

Stings

Insect stings are common, and for most people they aren't a serious problem. A small amount of redness or swelling at the site of the sting is expected. But some people have allergies to insects such as bees, and for them, a sting can be life-threatening. If after being stung a person develops hives (red, itchy bumps on the skin) or has trouble breathing, or if his tongue swells or he complains of not being able to swallow, you should call an ambulance or seek medical help immediately. These symptoms may mean that the person is having an allergic reaction, and this can be life-threatening.

Ask the person if they are carrying an epinephrine kit. If they are, assist them in making the simple injection.

Teeth Knocked Out

Sometimes children's (or adults') teeth get knocked out in accidents. It is important to try to save the tooth or the pieces that you can find, especially if it is a "big tooth." Place the tooth in a ziplock baggie in clean water or milk. The person should get dental attention right away. If a child gets an already loose baby tooth knocked out, or it simply comes out, have him or her rinse his or her mouth out with water. Save the tooth in a baggie for the parents and tell them what happened.

Trouble Breathing

A person having trouble breathing may be in serious trouble, but you can help. You have an emergency when a person is turning blue, cannot talk, or can talk only in one-word sentences. First, try to determine the cause:

- If the person has a history of asthma, treat it as an emergency.
- If the person got his or her breath knocked out while playing a game, wait to see if he or she recovers.
- If this is an older person who might have heart problems, ask him or her if the breathlessness is unusual.
- If the person appears to be choking, take immediate steps as described in the section on *Choking* (See page 175).

Other Minor Injuries

Small cuts, scrapes, or splinters can be handled by church personnel. But *for any injury to children, be sure to notify the parents and tell them exactly what happened and what you did to treat the injury.*

PUTTING TOGETHER A FIRST AID KIT

The mission of the faith community is service and ministry. Even though prevention of injuries is the best medicine, you never know when an emergency may arise. Having first aid kits in your facility allows you to give faster and better help to someone who might be hurt, and every facility should have at least one basic first aid kit. The larger your faith community, the more supplies you may wish to have on hand. Many of the items you need are inexpensive and can be purchased at your local drug store. A Sunday School class or youth group might want to donate a list of items as a service project.

Basic First Aid Supplies

Ideally, you will want to have kits in different areas of your facility—for example, one for the nursery, one for the sanctuary, and one for the gym. Each of these kits can contain a few additional items appropriate to the particular area—say, in the first aid kit for the gym, you might want to put a finger splint, more bandages and tape, and instant ice packs; in the kit for the sanctuary, smelling salts and an emesis bag (in case someone has a fit of vomiting) would be more appropriate.

A plastic container that seals securely makes a good holder for your kit. Select different colors, sizes, or shapes to help distinguish between your different kits. *Store your kits in a safe place away from children.*

While you may design particular kits for particular jobs, here is a list of basic first aid resources and supplies that you'll want in every kit:

Important phone numbers: Attach a phone list to each kit and next to each phone in your facility. Include the numbers for ambulance, fire and police departments, and the Poison Control Center.

Flashlight and/or penlight: A larger flashlight can be essential if the power goes off unexpectedly. A penlight is a smaller light that can be used to get a closer look at injuries, or can be used by a licensed professional to check the pupils of a person who may have suffered an injury to the head or some other problem. Be sure the batteries work and have an extra set in your kit. Flashlights should be inspected regularly—say, once a month.

Tweezers: Include tweezers in your kit to remove small splinters.

Small, sharp scissors: Scissors may be needed to cut tape, bandages, or perhaps even to cut clothing away to look at an injury.

Smelling salts: Small packets of smelling salts can be broken to let out a strong ammonia-like smell. They are placed underneath the nose of a person who has fainted to help revive him or her.

Bandages and pads of various sizes: Include bandages of all shapes and sizes in your kit. Be sure that any pads you buy are nonstick so they will be easy to remove at home, because they will probably be the most commonly used items in your kit. Keep them well stocked. Also stock packages of gauze pads (4 x 4's; 2 x 2's). These sizes of plain, sterile gauze are useful to clean or apply on wounds to stop bleeding.

Medical tape: Many different types of tape are available. Paper tape is easy on the skin, but it does not stick very well. Cloth tape is very sticky but can leave tape burns on the skin. An excellent type of tape is the clear hypoallergenic tape used in hospitals. It sticks well, doesn't leave tape marks, and rarely causes allergic reactions. You will need a couple of rolls of tape because it gets used up quickly, particularly in a sports first aid kit.

Elastic (Ace) bandages: (2", 4", 6"). These bandages can be used to help secure a dressing (other bandage) if you run out of tape. But their main use is for sprains or added support while playing sports. Use the smaller bandages for hands, arms, and ankles. Use the larger bandages for legs. Be sure to wash these bandages between uses or even discard them, depending on the amount of soiling that occurs. Do not encourage untrained people to "wrap" for sporting events, because improper wrapping can cause impaired blood flow and damage to tissues.

Finger splint: This item also is mainly for your sports kit. Jammed or injured fingers are common in contact sports, but can also happen during building projects. A splint is helpful until the injury can be examined by a professional.

Instant ice packs: These packs do not become cold until they are activated by breaking a substance inside the pack. Be careful to protect the skin when placing ice packs on an injury. Cold helps to decrease swelling and pain. Hot packs are also available.

Disposable gloves: To prevent the spread of bacteria, disease, and contact with bodily fluids (especially blood), all staff should wear gloves when treating bleeding injuries in an emergency. Staff will also need them to handle vomit. Be sure your nursery kit has plenty of disposable gloves. Check for Latex allergies among members of the congregation and children, because many gloves can cause serious reactions in those with latex sensitivity.

Empty squeeze bottle: An empty squeeze bottle can be filled with clean water and taken to the person on site to cleanse a wound when there's no running water nearby, or the person cannot be moved.

Clean wash cloths in baggies: Keep a supply of clean washcloths in your kit sealed inside ziplock bags. Washcloths may prove useful for cleansing an injury.

Sealable baggies: Extra plastic baggies are easy to store and can be filled with ice for instant ice packs if nothing else is available. They are also useful for storing teeth that may have fallen out (to give to parents).

Cotton balls: Sterile cotton balls are excellent for cleansing wounds. If no bandages are available, they can also be taped over small wounds as dressing.

Ipecac Syrup: This is the only essential medication for your first aid kit. It must be kept out of the reach of children. Ipecac Syrup is a liquid that causes vomiting immediately after it is taken. It is given to people who have taken certain types of poisons in order to make them vomit. Ipecac should ONLY be given when so instructed by a Poison Control Center, which is why you must keep the Poison Control Center number handy.

A note of caution here: If you were putting together a personal first aid kit for use in your home, you would likely include some additional items, such as over-the-counter ointments and other medications, like aspirin or Tylenol® (for aches, pain, or fever), antibiotic ointment (for minor cuts or scrapes), hydrocortisone cream (for minor rashes or itching), antacids (for upset stomach), and calamine lotion (for insect bits or itching).

But *unless you have a licensed professional coordinating your congregational health program, it is best not to keep medications in your first aid kit.* Some people may be allergic to certain medications that could make their condition worse. Small children could get into the kit and eat or drink something they shouldn't.

In any case, only a child's own parents should give the child medicine. For these and other reasons, *it is not the responsibility of church workers to give out medicine to others.* First aid should be just that—the first care you give to someone until they can get further help if needed. If people are seriously hurt, they should be seen as quickly as possible by their doctors or other health professionals for proper treatment.

MAKING DO

But what if you do not have the right supplies at the time you need them? Look around you. Be creative. Many common items you find in your church facility can act as a substitute in an emergency. For example:

- To splint an arm that is injured you can roll a magazine around the arm to help keep it still until the person can get medical attention
- Clean clothing from the lost and found box can be used to stop bleeding if no gauze or bandages are handy
- Plastic baggies from the nursery can be filled with ice cubes and made into ice packs
- That leftover bag of frozen peas that has been sitting in the church freezer for months makes a good and flexible ice pack, too (be sure to discard it after use!)

- Sports water bottles with the plastic straws attached are great for squirting away dirt and blood in order to see how bad an injury is when a sink or other water source is not handy

Once your first aid kits are put together:
- Tell your staff and volunteers where the first aid boxes are located. *Know where the first aid boxes are kept.* Not having to waste time looking for them can make a difference in an emergency situation.
- Put one person or a committee of people in charge of keeping the kits stocked with the needed items.
- Make a list of what is in each kit and fix it to the lid of the box. Place another copy of the list inside the box so that it can be taken to the store to buy replacement items.
- Be sure that each kit also has a list of emergency phone numbers that includes the ambulance service, police and fire departments, and the Poison Control Center.

Other Equipment

Walkers, canes, and especially crutches fit each person according to their height, walking ability, and other factors, so such devices are not practical to keep at the church.

But the church should own a *wheelchair*, particularly if you have many elderly people in your congregation. Wheelchairs can be used to transport people quickly and safely. If someone becomes weak or is injured, a wheelchair is a great asset.

There are several *ways to purchase a wheel chair cheaply:*
- Used wheelchairs may be purchased at hospital auction for a reasonable price.
- Family members often sell such equipment through newspaper ads when a loved one using them has died.
- Families are often happy to donate such items. Place an announcement in the church bulletin asking for donations of equipment that families no longer use.
- The parish nurse or congregational health coordinator could spearhead such a project.

Another piece of equipment you may want to have, especially if your congregation has a number of older adults, is an *oxygen tank*, along with someone who knows how to use it.

Before you purchase a tank, you'll want to discuss the situations when an oxygen tank can make a difference. The main reason to give a person oxygen is to treat shortness of breath that is not due to normal exercise or activity. Administering oxygen can be important first aid in an emergency situation while you are waiting for an ambulance to arrive.

Besides helping people who have become short of breath for unexplained causes, having an oxygen tank can help:

*   a person who already uses oxygen at home
*   a person who shows signs of a heart attack or stroke

Oxygen should be administered with care and by medically trained personnel. Improper use of oxygen could actually hurt a person by changing their blood gases or by masking a sign or symptom that a doctor might need to know about in order to make the right diagnosis.

Having an oxygen tank for emergency use also means that the congregation needs to explore the associated responsibilities and even dangers. Oxygen tanks must be inspected regularly, and staff must be trained in how to open the tank and how to use it. Oxygen tanks contain gas under pressure, which is flammable. The*re must be no smoking anywhere near the tank.*

In addition, a nasal cannula, mask, and tubing, or some other means of delivering the oxygen, must be readily available, and these items must be cleaned or replaced after use.

Some congregations may choose not to purchase an oxygen tank because of the considerable maintenance, risk, and cost of having one.

EMERGENCIES DURING WORSHIP SERVICES

It isn't uncommon for health-related emergencies to arise during the middle of a church service or other special event. Some people are afraid to show that they are feeling sick because they don't want to inconvenience anyone or make a fuss. Staff members should devise a plan of action for emergencies. Some larger churches have a nurse or doctor on call for every church service just to help with any possible emergency.

Let's look at an example. Bob, an elderly man with a history of high blood pressure, felt faint during the Sunday morning service, in the middle of the sermon. He was dizzy and sweaty and he looked pale, though no one noticed. Bob didn't want to say anything to his wife for fear of being noisy while the pastor was speaking, but he just kept feeling worse until he slumped over in the pew.

People helped him out of the sanctuary and into the hallway, while someone called an ambulance. The parish nurse was at his side until the paramedics arrived. She recognized the warning signs of a stroke and knew that Bob had to be seen by a doctor.

The sooner these signs are reported, the better the chance of early and successful treatment. Bob was found to have blocked arteries in his neck. Surgery corrected the problem. Now he's doing fine because he listened to his body's warning signals and got help with the encouragement of his church friends. If he hadn't been in a congregation that knew how to handle such emergencies, his story could have had a less happy ending. (Your church library should own *Your Body's Red Light Warning Signals: Medical Tips That May Save Your Life*, and we recommend this book to members of your congregation; see reference below.)

Find out if your congregation has one or more qualified members who are willing to "take call" during church services or activities. A plan for handling health-related emergencies should be approved by the congregation. Members who are licensed health care professionals (such as doctors and nurses or physician's assistants) may wish to organize themselves and assign one of their group to each church event, using a monthly calendar, on a rotating basis. Volunteers must be certified in CPR. The health care professionals could provide this and other necessary training to the volunteers.

People on call *must* be in the service or at the event they are assigned so that emergencies can be treated promptly. The congregation should be made aware that a health care professional, or at least a trained volunteer, will be on call at each service or event.

People should be encouraged to go to the back of the room or out into the hallway if they are not feeling well. If Bob knew that, he'd have received treatment faster than he did. An usher may be summoned for assistance in locating the health care worker or volunteer on call if the worker is not right on the spot.

Many churches use a silent pager system for parents with children in the nursery. The nurse or doctor on call could be given such a pager that could be used to notify him or her when or if assistance is needed.

REFERENCE

Shulman, Neil B., Birge, Jack B., and Ahn, Joon: *Your Body's Red Light Warning Signals: Medical Tips that May Save Your Life* Dell Publishing Company, N. Y., 1999.

SEVEN

PROMOTING HEALTH IN YOUR CONGREGATION

In order to promote health in your church, you must first come to a common understanding of what is meant by health. As we see it, the word *health* refers to a state or condition of the body, mind, and spirit that allows a person to engage in life at its fullest. To minister to your own health or to someone else's, you must attend to physical, emotional, intellectual, social, and spiritual well-being. A comprehensive congregational health program attends to each of these areas, recognizing that as we live and experience them, these are not distinct categories but rather integrated aspects of the whole person.

SETTING A FOCUS ON HEALTH

The traditional model for illness concentrates more or less exclusively on the treatment of disease. Though disease prevention and management will be part of your focus, the congregational health model goes further. Your health ministry will urge members of your congregation to make positive choices on issues of health and wellness.

Such choices might include participation in:

- health screenings
- healthy lifestyle classes

• health education seminars
• disease prevention or management workshops

The program you develop must address the specific needs of your congregation. Their needs will vary depending on the size and composition of the congregation. If your congregation has many young families, you will want to emphasize issues of prenatal health, parenting skills, and concerns for childhood safety. Congregations with many older adults will spend more time focusing on issues of transition to retirement and to specific health concerns of aging.

The best way to determine the health needs and interests of your congregation is to ask the members. One way is to hold open group discussions in which members share their ideas and concerns. The down side to this approach is that some people who participate at a later date in health-related activities may feel shy about offering planning ideas.

Another approach you might try is a written survey. Write it as clearly and simply as you can, then distribute and collect the survey during or following the service. Or, you might distribute the questionnaire through a monthly health ministry newsletter.

Here is a sample survey, which you can modify according to your needs.

Once you know what people want and need, you'll want to pick specific topics to explore and health activities to promote. From our suggestions on the next several pages, you can lay a foundation for your health program and build from there. We wish only to give you the tools. Your survey will help you decide which of these areas should be your top priorities.

COMMON AREAS FOR DISCUSSION AND PROGRAMS

Environment

Environmental conditions significantly affect health in a number of ways. Some environmental effects can take years to show up in the onset of particular diseases. People have to become alert to potential dangers in their environment, so that, with the help of community resources, they can work to eliminate them.

SAMPLE CONGREGATIONAL HEALTH SURVEY

In planning our health ministry programs, we want to know what topics or activities are of interest to you. Please complete this brief survey so that we can better serve you. After all, our programs will be for YOUR HEALTH!

Circle your answer.
Gender: Male   Female
Age: 8–12   13–18   19–24   25–34   35–44   45–54   55–64   65+
Describe your health: Excellent   Good   Fair   Poor
Do you have a physician or other health care provider?   Yes   No

Please circle all topics that interest you for future health programming:

Environmental Health	Exercise
Immunizations	Mental Health
Leisure Time Activities	Men's Health
Women's Health	Children's Health
Mature Adults' Health	Safety
Sexual Health	Parenting
Retirement Planning	Senior Health
Substance Abuse	Tobacco Use
Weight Management	Cancer
Hypertension	Heart Health
Alzheimer's Disease	Stroke
Prostate Health	Osteoporosis

Other topics of interest?_____

Please list your top three health priorities:_____

_____

Comments?_____

_____

Thank you for participating in this survey!
—Your Health Ministry Team

Environmental toxins may come from many sources—noise, air, water, or land pollution, chemical toxins, and radiation. To help the members of your congregation understand the risks, *you can organize workshops on safeguarding the home, workplace, school, and church.* You may want to start with the church as a model for the other spaces.

Specific issues will easily come to mind:

- Do you still permit smoking on church grounds? Try banning smoking anywhere on church property. Your action would lessen members' exposure to second-hand smoke, which can cause cancer. It might also encourage members to quit smoking, which would be a big victory for your health program!
- Is your ventilation system clean and effective? Remember that dirty systems cause serious air pollution.
- Does your church space have adequate lighting? If not, add more lighting and use incandescent bulbs instead of fluorescent tubes whenever possible. Accidents are less likely to happen where the lighting is good.

Exercise

- Keeping physically active and establishing a regular exercise program are necessary for *everyone* in the congregation, from the youngest to the oldest members. The church can serve as a convenient, nonthreatening center to get people started and to help them maintain an exercise program. It shouldn't be hard to sell such a program. Look at the benefits:
- Increased flexibility, strength, and endurance
- Decreased risk for some diseases (cancer, heart disease, diabetes)
- Improved sleep and rest
- Stronger bones
- Increased life expectancy
- Better weight management
- Better self-image
- More energy

- Better stress management
- Decreased depression and anxiety

As if all that weren't enough, physical activity is fun, especially when you're working with others. The ingredients of a successful exercise program are not difficult to achieve.

- First, exercise must be regular. If your church decides to offer an aerobic class, offer it at least twice a week at the same time each week. No exceptions! Challenge participants who exercise on their own to work out three or more times per week.
- To be effective, and increase heart rate, aerobic activity requires a minimum of twenty minutes of sustained exercise. Participants are encouraged to increase their exercise time to thirty or forty-five minutes per workout.
- In addition to aerobic exercise, strength training is key to any exercise plan. Strength training increases muscle mass, which results in more effective exercise and a body more able and eager to do its job.
- Maintaining motivation to exercise can be difficult, but partici- pants can encourage one another to stay on course with the program.
- Finally, making exercising fun will keep participants actively involved.

Walking is a form of exercise that is particularly suited for con- gregational participation. After all, Jesus serves as a wonderful role model for the many benefits of walking. (Moses did his share, too.) Other than a good pair of shoes, walking requires no specialized equipment. There is no need for a special instructor, either, and walking is an exercise that you can do anywhere—in the neighbor- hood, in a park, on the mall, or even in the church itself.

Some people enjoy walking in groups, others use walking as a chance to get time to themselves. Walking exercises the whole body, including the heart, and offers the least risk of injury.

Once you have some people who want to walk together, let them decide where they want to walk. If the weather's nice and the neigh- borhood friendly, people may want to go outside to enjoy the scenery. If the weather is bad, you can walk laps at your recreation center or at the indoor shopping mall.

Tell people to be realistic. They should begin walking for just ten minutes a day and gradually increase to thirty minutes or more every day—they will be amazed by the results! Most people, whatever their condition, can benefit from some exercise, however light. But keep in mind that participants over thirty-five years old, or people with health problems, should check with their doctors or other health care providers before they begin an exercise program.

Immunizations

Immunizations are essential to protecting the lives of children by reducing the risk of disability and even death from many infectious diseases. The success of the immunization program, however, has made the public and even some clinicians complacent, so that children do not always receive the immunization shots they need.

Encourage families to order a free copy of a pamphlet developed by the Centers for Disease Control (CDC). This guide provides essential information about vaccinations in a readable format. The chart on the next page is from this guide and provides a reference for the recommended childhood immunization schedule. To order your copy of *Parent's Guide to Childhood Immunization* online, go to www.cdc.gov/nip/publications/Parents-Guide/default.htm You can call the National Immunization Information Hotline for further immunization information at 1–800–232–2522 (English) or at 1–800–232–0233 (Spanish).

Leisure Time Activities: Play and Laughter

Today more than ever we sometimes forget what happens when it's all work and no play. That's why we need reminding. In order to do just that, your ministry may want to promote leisure-time activities, play, and laughter.

Again, let's look at the benefits. People who know how to laugh and play reap benefits of body and mind. Some of the known benefits include:

IMMUNIZATION SCHEDULE

Vaccines work best when they are given at certain ages. For example, measles vaccine is not usually given until a child is at least a year old. it if is given earlier than that, it may not work as well. On the other hand, T TaP vaccine should be given over a period of time, in a series of properly-spaced doses.

The following chart shows the routine childhood immunization schedule. It tells you:

What childhood vaccines are recommended, and the ages they should be given.

Read across the chart to see how many doses of each vaccine are recommended, and when. Read down the chart to see which vaccines are given at specificl ages.

A circle means the vaccine should be given at that age. A bar means it may be geven at an point over a periof of time. For example, the first dose may be given at any time between 6 and 18 months.

	Birth	1 Month	2 Months	4 Months	6 Months	12 Months	15 Months	18 Months	4–6 Years
Hepatitus B		1	2			3			
Hb			1	2	3	4			
Polio			1	2	3				4
D TaP			1	2	3	4			5
Pneumo			1	2	3	4			
MMR						1			2
Varicella						1			

Hepatitis A Two doses at least 6 months apart.
Recommended in selected areas for children over 2 years of age.

This chart is based on the Ummunization schedule recommended by CDC, the American Academy of Pediatrics, and the American Academy of Family Physicians.

- pain reduction
- decreased anxiety
- improved mood
- ability to relax

Here are some of the things you might do to help your congregation reap these benefits:

- Organize softball, basketball or volleyball games. By doing so, you invite and encourage people to exercise and enjoy fellowship. Even people who might not ordinarily participate in activities may do so in a congregational setting, where the focus is on having a good time together rather than on competition.
- Sponsor hiking, rock climbing, or bicycling groups.
- Make a list of other possibilities that represent the interests of the congregation.

Of course, one can also have a good time without exercising. A group might:

- Develop a collection of silly or humorous videotapes, DVDs, audiotapes, or books that people could enjoy at the church or at home.
- Offer a health workshop on the benefits of laughter (a good way to lighten up the congregation on a long winter's night).
- Play and laughter aren't sin. Remind members of the congregation (and yourself) that having fun is part of the prescription for a healthy life.

MEN'S HEALTH

The average American man, including the men in your church, will especially benefit from a health promotion program. Too often, men don't seek help until their symptoms force them to seek it, and then it's sometimes too late for the most effective treatment and cure.

A good men's health program will encourage positive health habits and early detection of disease. That means a man must pay attention to his own body, and know how to get medical help and advice when he needs it.

The web site at http://www.healthfinder.gov offers an excellent place to begin your research. Once your group has learned some of the basic information to be found there, consider the following topics for development and discussion:

Screening Tests for Men: These tests include blood chemistries, blood pressure, cholesterol, colon examination, dental examination, digital rectal examination, eye examination, prostate-specific antigen (PSA) test, sexually transmitted diseases, skin examination, testicular examination, total thyroxine (T4) or thyroid-stimulating hormone (TSH), transferrin saturation, urinalysis. Your parish nurse may be able to help you set up monitoring programs for your men's health group.

Sexual Health: Fertility, impotence, safe sex, testicular health, sexually transmitted diseases

Cancer: Prevention, treatment, recovery

Heart Health: Prevention, treatment, recovery

Prostate Health: Prevention, treatment, recovery

Mental Health: Types, causes, prevention, recovery

Smoking and Tobacco: Dangers, how to stop

Drug and Alcohol Use: Dangers. How to stop.

Mental Health

Nearly half the population will experience a mental disorder in their lifetimes. Add to that the family members and friends who feel the impact of mental disorders, and you can see the importance of this health topic.

The social stigma of mental illness sometimes blocks opportunities for open discussion but that makes discussion all the more important. Your congregational health program can provide speakers and discussion groups that can debunk the myths of mental illness, share facts, provide hope through new treatment options, and offer support to those affected by mental illness.

Suggested topics for mental health programs include:

- *Mood Disorders*, such as depression and bipolar depression
- *Anxiety Disorders*, such as post-traumatic stress disorder, phobias, generalized anxiety disorder, obsessive-compulsive disorder, and panic
- Substance Abuse
- Schizophrenia
- *Alzheimer's Disease* and other organic brain disorders
- Suicide
- *Childhood Conditions*, such as autism, attention deficit hyperactivity disorder
- Issues of Grief and Loss
- Building Self-Esteem
- Effectively handling Developmental Transitions

Through discussion of such topics, you can end the stigma. Getting started takes some planning, but it's not complicated. Encourage mental health professionals who worship in your congregation to get discussions going. If no one is available in the congregation, talk to your local mental health association or mental health clinic. Most professionals welcome the opportunity to move people toward hope and better care.

Since treatment issues are usually beyond the scope of the church health program, you'll need outside resources. On the Internet these organizations can help:

National Alliance for the Mentally Ill (NAMI) – http://www.nami.org/
National Mental Health Association (NMHA) – http://www.nmha.org/
National Institute of Mental Health (NIMH) – http://www.nimh.nih.gov/

NUTRITION

Nothing is more basic to good health than good nutrition. At the same time, a poor diet is associated with weakened immune function, reduced energy, minor ailments, and serious, sometimes chronic illnesses. Bad diets contribute to diseases such as diabetes, coronary heart disease, stroke, and some cancers.

The principles of a healthy diet aren't a mystery, but with the many "fad" diets, eating right can seem complicated and hard to understand. Work with a nutrition educator to develop a healthy eating program at your church.

Many nutritionists follow the Food Guide Pyramid developed by the U. S. Department of Agriculture. This food guide recommends that the daily diet contain six to eleven portions of cereal foods (bread, cereal, rice, and pasta), two to four portions of fruits, three to five portions of vegetables, two to three portions of meats (meat, poultry, fish, dry beans, eggs, and nuts), and 2–3 of dairy foods (milk, yogurt, and cheese), and the sparse use of fats, oils, and sweets.

Whether or not you follow the Food Guide Pyramid, everyone can benefit from these dietary suggestions:

- Eat a diet that includes a variety of whole grains, beans, nuts, seeds, vegetables, and fresh fruits.
- Increase fiber in your diet.
- Reduce sugar in your diet.
- Reduce salt in your diet.
- Decrease the intake of saturated fats and cholesterol.
- Choose lean meats, and low fat dairy products.
- Eat adequate though not excessive amounts of protein.
- Avoid processed, packaged, and prepared foods containing added fat, salt, and sugar.
- Drink eight eight-ounce servings of water per day (adjust if on fluid restrictions).

Many experts argue that too few Americans get the nutrients they need through diet alone. Multi-nutrient supplements can fill that gap. Invite a qualified nutritionist to lead a discussion about this issue.

SAFETY

By creating a safe space for your congregation you also create a model that members can apply to their homes. The payoff will come in the form of accidents prevented and lives saved.

The National Safety Council (http://www.nsc.org/pus/fsh/archive/homesaf.htm) recommends that you have on hand, in an easily accessible location, the following resources and devices to make your congregation or home a safe place:

- List of emergency telephone numbers, including 911 and a crisis hotline number, addresses and directions to the hospital emergency room and the Poison Control Center
- Fire extinguishers
- Emergency evacuation plan(s)
- Functioning smoke alarms
- First-aid kits
- Working flashlights that are accessible
- Survival kits
- Carbon monoxide alarms
- Grab bars and slip-resistant mats in showers and bathtubs
- Ground-fault circuit interrupters
- Tagged water and power lines
- Safety glass
- Handrails and gates
- Tested appliances
- Illumination of entrances, stairwells, and hallways
- One-step stools
- Safety goggles

CHILDPROOFING

Childproofing is a safety issue that deserves special consideration. You don't want children hurt in easily preventable accidents. Here are a few tips on childproofing:

- If your church offers a nursery program and cribs are available, be certain that the cribs meet recognized safety standards.

- Do not place the cribs next to windows because cords from blinds and drapery can cause hazards.
- Avoid the use of mobiles and crib gyms because after the age of five months these toys can pose a risk to infants.
- Eliminate small toys or objects that a child may swallow, because these objects pose a choking risk.
- Place childproof latches on cabinets and safety plugs in outlets.
- Car safety seats should meet all recognized safety standards and be installed properly.
- In the home setting, observe gun safety.

DROWNING

Children under the age of five and men fifteen to twenty-four years of age are particularly at risk for drowning. Close supervision of children is critical. Be sure that group leaders receive training in basic cardiopulmonary resuscitation techniques.

For each age group there are particular dangers:

- Infants: Inadequate supervision in the bathtub is usually the cause of drowning.
- Older Children: Accidents in swimming pools are the primary cause of drowning.
- Adolescents and adults: Drowning often happens during recreational activities on bodies of water, and alcohol may be involved. When a church group takes part in water activities, counsel the participants on, and stress the importance of, not drinking alcohol near the water.

FALLS

Children can fall off furniture, down stairs, or even off buildings, but good supervision will prevent these falls from happening.

- Be certain that windows and doors are locked and secured so that children don't wander toward open windows or other dangerous places.

- Bicycles can cause serious falls. Be sure that whenever children ride, they are wearing helmets. You might want to organize a bicycle rodeo that encourages children to wear helmets and decorate their bicycles with stickers that emphasize the importance of helmets. The rodeo could also teach bicycle safety and could be fun.

Older adults are at great risk for falls that can occur during quite ordinary activities, like walking, or getting out of a chair. At church, as in the home, reduce the risk of falls with:

- good lighting
- nonstick traction strips on flooring
- handrailings
- Avoid the use of loose rugs and secure all electrical cords.

In parts of the country with harsh winter weather, clear all walkways and parking areas of ice and snow. Valet parking for older adults or congregational members who require special assistance will reduce the risk of falls.

FIRES AND BURNS

The fourth leading cause of death from injury is burns and fires, with 1.4 million injuries and approximately 4,000 deaths in the United States each year. *Smoking in or around the church or home is a known risk factor for fire and burns.* Matches, lighters, and flammable materials must be kept in a secure place and away from children.

Here are some additional suggestions for making your congregation as fireproof as possible:

- Install an adequate number of smoke detectors in locations that are near potential sources of smoke. Be certain that the detectors are functional and that the batteries are fresh.
- Place fire extinguishers in any potential fire hazard areas.
- Plan an escape route in case of fire and practice the evacuation procedures for the church regularly.

- Post the fire escape plan as a reminder to church members.
- Your local fire department can probably offer assistance in developing a fire safety program for the church or home.

MOTOR VEHICLE SAFETY

Encourage all members of your church to use seat belts every time they are in a motor vehicle. *Besides being the law in most states, using the seat belt saves lives.*

Use of approved child restraint systems for infants and children is critical. Be sure the restraint is fitted for the child and is properly installed.

Of course, drinking and driving do not mix. Avoid the use of alcohol at all church sponsored events. A special program on the risks of drinking while under the influence of alcohol is appropriate for the youth group.

POISONING

The third leading cause of injury in the United States is poisoning, with children under five years of age at greatest risk. Here are some ways to prevent poisoning:

- Keep potentially harmful chemicals or medications away from children and in secure areas.
- Maintain fresh one-ounce bottles of ipecac syrup in a place that is readily accessible. Use the ipecac syrup only under the instruction of the local Poison Control Center.
- Be sure that the telephone number of the local poison control center is posted next to all telephones.

SEX AND STDS

God created humans as sexual beings and sexual health is an important part of our overall well-being. As a member of a health ministry, you have a wonderful opportunity to promote sexual health in a safe and non-threatening environment.

With all due respect for specific religious teachings and beliefs, we suggest educational activities for specific groups, such as women, men, adolescents, or older adults.

During discussion involving groups, a member may share that he/she is currently being sexually abused or has been violated in the past. It is critical that you support this person emotionally and spiritually. It's also important that you assist him/her in locating professional and legal help. In most congregations, the issues of abuse (sexual, physical, and emotional) require referrals outside of the church.

Spiritual support and understanding, along with the support of outside help, will provide a strong foundation to build toward recovery for members who have experienced abuse.

Sexually transmitted diseases (STDs) are a significant public health problem in the United States. STDs include:

- chlamydia
- gonorrhea
- pelvic inflammatory disease
- syphilis
- genital herpes and warts
- human papilloma virus
- hepatitis
- HIV infection

Primary prevention of STD can be acieved by launching health education programs directed at preventing infection. Have discussions about abstaining from sex, or, if your congregation is comfortable, about safe sex; about injecting drugs; and about other high-risk behaviors. Emphasize the importance of maintaining a monogamous sexual relationship and of proper use of condoms. In some communities, STDs have become an urgent, even epidemic problem. Your congregation can help protect people from becoming part of that problem.

You must accept the possibility that some members of your congregation are already infected. For them, you must teach "secondary prevention"—that is, early detection and treatment. That's the next best thing to not getting infected in the first place.

Stress Management

Stress is a normal and natural fact of the human experience. Everyone in the congregation relates to stress on a personal level. And these days we also share some measure of national stress.

Stress in itself is neither good nor bad. It is a part of life and effective people find ways to live with it. But when it overwhelms a person, stress becomes dangerous. It can even become a killer.

Conditions associated with stress include:

- high blood pressure
- depression
- ulcers
- colds
- cardiovascular disease,
- asthma
- headaches

Through *stress management programs* you can teach the members of your congregation about the nature and sources of stress, the effects of stress on health, and ways to reduce and manage the stress in their lives. Among the resources available to such programs of stress management and reduction are:

- prayer
- breathing
- meditation
- relaxation
- imagery
- exercise
- time management

You can find further material on the subject of stress relief in Chapter 9 of *The Heart of the Matter: The African American's Guide to Heart Disease, Heart Treatment, and Heart Wellness.*

Programs for selected groups such as caregivers or women are often especially helpful. You might also develop stress relief programs for stressful times of the year such as the Christmas season.

SUBSTANCE USE AND ABUSE

This is admittedly a tough issue. The subject of alcohol and drug use covers the range of nonuse, use, misuse, abuse, dependence, and recovery.

Misuse of a substance progresses to *abuse* when a person continues to use the substance even after he or she has begun to experience health or behavioral problems that result from the drug.

Dependence on a substance involves *withdrawal symptoms* if the substance is withheld, or *tolerance* when more substance is required for the desired effect.

Though it is beyond the scope of most church health programs to treat alcohol or drug abuse, you can educate the congregation about these forms of abuse. *By providing the basic facts related to alcohol and drug abuse, you may provide the stimulus for members to seek help.*

A simple screening tool called *the CAGE Questionnaire* will help you assess for alcoholism. Answering "yes" to two or more questions indicates probable concern and the person should be referred for additional assessment by a health professional specializing in substance abuse. The questions include:

Have you ever felt you ought to *Cut* down on your drinking?

Have people *Annoyed* you by criticizing your drinking?

Have you ever felt bad or *Guilty* about your drinking?

Have you ever had a drink first thing in the morning to steady your nerves or get rid of a hangover *(Eye-opener)*?*

Besides having a list of qualified referral sources in your community, you can find a wealth of information through the National Clearinghouse for Alcohol and Drug Information at http://www.health.org/

Recognize that recovering from substance abuse is an ongoing process and that relapses are expected. Participation in support groups such as Alcoholics Anonymous helps promote recovery.

---

*Ewing, JA: *JAMA* 252: 1905, 1984.

Substance use and abuse affects the abuser's entire social network including family members, friends, and co-workers. Support programs within the church for friends and family of abusers are an important addition to your health programming.

TOBACCO USE

If you develop an effective smoking cessation (Stop Smoking!) program in your church, a lot of people will benefit. Any tobacco use is dangerous not only to smokers but also to those exposed to second-hand smoke. Here's why everyone should stop smoking and chewing tobacco:

- About 430,000 deaths are attributed to cigarette smoking each year.
- Approximately one of every two lifelong smokers will eventually die of smoking.
- People who smoke are at greater risk for heart disease, stroke, respiratory disease, osteoporosis, and lung and ovarian cancer.
- Pregnant women who smoke have double the rate of miscarriage as those who do not smoke.
- Children living with parents who smoke have significantly more respiratory illnesses, such as asthma, than those living with nonsmokers.
- People who quit smoking report feeling healthier and better about themselves.
- Even people who have smoked for a long time can improve their health and extend their lives by stopping and allowing the body to heal.

A successful smoking cessation program begins with the participant's sincere desire to give up smoking. The smoker must make the decision. It won't help to drag a person into a program against his will, merely by force of group pressure.

Once your group is formed, assist participants in declaring a specific day on which they will quit smoking. Designating a "quit date" brings people closer to actually quitting.

Discuss whether he or she plans to use nicotine replacement therapy (gum, patches, and inhalers). These products are available over-the-counter and assist in reducing withdrawal symptoms.

The participant must expect withdrawal symptoms when she stops using nicotine. These symptoms may include anger, anxiety, depressed mood, and difficulty concentrating. These symptoms will subside within three to four weeks after the last cigarette. Craving nicotine and increased appetite lasts longer, usually months. The ministry will want to provide strong, sympathetic support to people experiencing withdrawal symptoms.

Identify a list of alternative behaviors to smoking, so that the ex-smoker will have something else to do when the urge to smoke occurs.

- Chew gum, eat plenty of fruits and vegetables.
- Play sports, exercise.
- Buy new clothes, change your hair style.
- Reward yourself for each day you don't smoke.

Help the smoker realize that everything changes when he or she quits smoking. Especially significant is the change in social network. Ex-smokers may no longer want to spend time with people who still smoke.

The supportive environment of a caring church community can assist the person who wants to quit smoking. Use of a buddy system can help as can prayer and turning to God for support.

The government website at http://www.healthfinders.gov/ offers many suggestions and links when you search under "smoking cessation."

Remember that many successful former smokers required several attempts before they actually quit smoking. So keep encouraging participants, even the backsliders!

WEIGHT MANAGEMENT

The number of overweight Americans keeps increasing. Health care providers are most concerned with those people who are considered *obese,* which means they are at least twenty percent above the upper limit of normal weight according to their age, sex, and height.

Obesity is associated with:

• diabetes
• increased blood pressure
• heart disease
• high cholesterol
• some forms of cancer
• stroke, gallbladder disease
• arthritis in the weight-bearing joints

Weight loss reduces the health risks associated with obesity and also promotes better physical and psychological health.

Successful weight loss programs are measured not so much by the amount of weight that is lost as by how close one gets to a decided *target weight.* "Yo-yo" dieting, with weight loss and gain, simply doesn't work in the long run. Instead, a person should *focus on healthy eating and exercise.*

Nutrition can seem complicated at first and, to keep it simple, you may want a nutrition expert to lead your program. Be sure that everyone who plans to participate gets an o.k. from his or her health care provider.

The elements of a successful weight management program include:

• a healthy eating plan
• gradual change
• behavioral interventions
• healthy shopping and cooking
• exercise

WOMEN'S HEALTH

In the American culture, women tend to assume responsibility for managing the health of the entire family. But that can mean that the woman's own health gets overlooked. You can change this situation by creating a comprehensive program that addresses the health needs of the women in your congregation. For an excellent web site specific to women, go to http://www.4woman.gov/faq/index.htm. Another excellent resource is *Our Bodies, Ourselves: For the New Century.*

Consider the following topics for development and discussion:

- Screening Tests for Women: blood chemistries, blood pressure, breast examination and mammography, cholesterol, colon examination, dental examination, digital recto-vaginal examination, eye examination, pap smear, sexually transmitted diseases, skin examination, total thyroxine (T4) or thyroid-stimulating hormone (TSH), urinalysis
- Sexual Health: Fertility, pregnancy, contraception, safe sex, sexually transmitted diseases
- Menopause
- Cancer
- Osteoporosis
- Heart Health
- Mental Health
- Smoking and Tobacco
- Drug and Alcohol Use

MORE IDEAS FOR PROMOTING HEALTH IN YOUR CONGREGATION

If you think back to last year, you can probably recall at least one national health observance. For some, it might be "American Heart Month" in February or "The Great American Smoke Out," which happens in November. And there are many others, as you'll see from our list below.

You might want to organize your church health program around the federal government's calendar that lists the various national observances. Of course, no church would try to recognize each observance! You could challenge the congregation to focus on one observance each month.

Here's the current calendar (to check on updates, go to this web site: http://www.healthfinder.gov/library/nho/nhoyear.htm)

NATIONAL HEALTH OBSERVANCES

January
Cervical Cancer Month
National Birth Defects Prevention Month
National Eye Care Month
National Glaucoma Awareness Month
National Volunteer Blood Donor Week
Sight Saving Sabbath (Second Week)
Healthy Weight Week (Third Week)

February
American Heart Month
Low Vision Awareness Month
National Children's Dental Health Month
Wise Health Consumer Month
Cardiac Rehabilitation Week (First Week)
National Burn Awareness Week (First Week)
National Girls and Women in Sports Day (First Wednesday)
National Child Passenger Safety Awareness Week (Second Week)
National Children of Alcoholics Week (Second Week)
National Condom Day (February 14)

March
American Red Cross Month
Mental Retardation Awareness Month
National Chronic Fatigue Syndrome Awareness Month
National Colorectal Cancer Awareness Month
National Eye Donor Month
National Kidney Month
Workplace Eye Health and Safety Awareness Month
Save Your Vision Week (First Week)
National School Breakfast Week (First Week)
Pulmonary Rehabilitation Week (Second Week)
Brain Awareness Week (Second Week)
National Inhalants and Poisons Awareness Week (Third Week)

National Poison Prevention Week (Third Week)
American Diabetes Alert
World Tuberculosis Day

April

Alcohol Awareness Month
Cancer Control Month
Counseling Awareness Month
IBS (Irritable Bowel Syndrome) Awareness Month
National Autism Awareness Month
National Child Abuse Prevention Month
National Occupational Therapy Month
National STD Awareness Month
National Youth Sports Safety Month
Sports Eye Safety Month
Women's Eye Health and Safety Month
National Building Safety Week (First Week)
National Public Health Week (First Week)
Kick Butts Day (First Wednesday)
Alcohol-free Weekend (First Full Weekend)
World Health Day
YMCA Health Kids Day
National Organ and Tissue Donor Awareness Week (Third
    Week)
National Minority Cancer Awareness Week (Third Week)
National Infants Immunization Week (Fourth Week)
WalkAmerica (Last Full Weekend)

May

Asthma and Allergy Awareness Month
Better Hearing and Speech Month
Better Sleep Month
Clean Air Month
Correct Posture Month
Hepatitis Awareness Month

Huntington's Disease Awareness Month
National Arthritis Month
National Digestive Diseases Awareness Month
Skin Cancer Awareness Month
Tuberous Sclerosis Awareness Month
National High Blood Pressure Education Month
National Melanoma/Skin Cancer Detection and Prevention
    Month
National Mental Health Month
National Neurofibromatosis Month
National Osteoporosis Prevention Month
National Sight-Saving Month
National Stroke Awareness Month
National Teen Pregnancy Prevention Month
National Trauma Awareness Month
Older Americans Month
National Anxiety Disorders Screening Day (May 2)
National SAFE KIDS Week (First Week)
Mother's Day Comes Early For Too Many of Our Nation's Teens
    (Mother's Day)
National Suicide Awareness Week (Second Week)
Food Allergy Awareness Week (Second Week)
Childhood Depression Awareness Day (May 7)
National Mental Health Counseling Week (Second Week)
National Running and Fitness Week (Third Week)
National Alcohol-and Other Drug-Related Birth Defects Week
    (Third Week)
National Stuttering Awareness Week (Third Week)
National Employee Health and Fitness Day (May 17)
National Emergency Medical Services Week (Third Week)
Buckle Up America! Week (Third Week)
National Missing Children's Day (May 25)
National Senior Health and Fitness Day (May 30)
World "No Tobacco" Day (May 31)

June
Fireworks Safety Month (through July 4)
National Safety Month
National Scleroderma Awareness Month
Vision Research Month
National Cancer Survivors Day (First Sunday)
National Aphasia Awareness Week (First Week)
National Headache Awareness Week (First Week)
National Men's Health Week (Second Week)
Helen Keller Deaf-Blind Awareness Week (Fourth Week)
Light the Night for Sight (End of June)
Eye Safety Awareness Week (End of June, including July 4)
National Sobriety Checkpoint Week (End of June, including July 4)

July
Fireworks Safety Month
Hemochromatosis Screening Awareness Month
National Therapeutic Recreation Week (Second Week)

August
Cataract Awareness Month
Spinal Muscular Atrophy Awareness Month
World Breastfeeding Week (First Week)

September
Baby Safety Month
National Sickle Cell Month
Children's Eye Health and Safety Month
Cold and Flu Campaign
Gynecologic Cancer Awareness Month
Health Aging Month
Leukemia Awareness Month
National Cholesterol Month
National Food Safety Education Month
National Pediculosis Prevention Month

Ovarian Cancer Awareness Month
National 5–A-Day Week (Second Week)
National Reye's Syndrome Week (Third Week)
Prostate Cancer Awareness Week (Third Week)
National Rehabilitation Week (Third Week)
Ulcer Awareness Week (Third Week)
Family Health and Fitness Days USA (End September)

October

Auto Battery Safety Month
Celiac Sprue Awareness Month
Child Health Month
Domestic Violence Awareness Month
Family Health Month
Health Literacy Month
Healthy Lung Month
National Breast Cancer Awareness Month
National Campaign for Healthier Babies Month
National Dental Hygiene Month
National Family Sexuality Education Month
National Liver Awareness Month
National Lupus Awareness Month
National Physical Therapy Month
National Spina Bifida Prevention Month
National Spinal Health Month
Rett Syndrome Awareness Month
Sudden Infant Death Syndrome Awareness Month
Talk About Prescriptions Month
Child Health Day (Early October)
Mental Illness Awareness Week (First Week)
National Depression Screening Day (First Week)
National Fire Prevention Week (Second Week)
Walk a Child to School Week (Second Week)
National Adult Immunization Awareness Week (Second Week)
National School Lunch Week (Third Week)

National Hepatitis Awareness Week (Third Week)
National Radon Action Week (Third Week)
National Health Education Week (Third Week)
World Food Day (Mid October)
National Infection Control Week (Third Week)
National Mammography Day (Mid October)
National Red Ribbon Celebration (Fourth Week)

November
American Diabetes Month
Diabetic Eye Disease Month
National Alzheimer's Awareness Month
National Epilepsy Month
National Hospice Month
National Marrow Awareness Week (First Week)
National Osteopathic Medicine Week (Second Week)
Great American Smoke Out (November 15)
GERD Awareness Week (Third Week)
National Adoption Week (Third Week)

December
National Drunk and Drugged Driving Prevention Month
Safe Toys and Gifts Month
World AIDS Day (December 1)
National Aplastic Anemia Awareness Week (First Week)

To take an example, for "National High Blood Pressure Education Month" in May you could organize blood pressure screening with your team of professional volunteers. *Be prepared to refer those with high readings to their primary health care provider.*

Follow up this activity with a health seminar that describes high blood pressure and its associated health concerns and treatment options. You'll come up with other programs for other items listed on the calendar.

Over the years, you will further develop and expand those topics that generate interest in your congregation, and you will almost certainly find new themes. Your members will come to expect certain health-related activities each year.

Remember to *request free pamphlets and materials from the national clearinghouses.* Also, check your local health associations and the public library for materials and audiovisual aids.

Be creative and have fun. Remember that your congregation's health is at stake!

REFERENCES

Hudson, Hilton M. and Stern, Herbert: *The Heart of the Matter: The African American's Guide to Heart Disease, Heart Treatment, and Heart Wellness.* Roscoe, IL: Hilton Publishing Company, 2000.

The Boston Women's Health Collective: *Our Bodies, Our Selves: For the New Century.* New York: Simon & Schuster, 1998.

PART THREE
COPING WITH
HARD TIMES

EIGHT

LIVING WITH CHRONIC ILLNESS

There are probably people in your congregation who have long-term or "chronic" health problems. In this chapter, you will learn what chronic illness means, both in medical terms and from the point of view of the patient.

"ACUTE" AND "CHRONIC" ILLNESS

Medical professionals distinguish between two kinds of illnesses—"acute" and "chronic." *Acute illness* is a condition or sickness that is temporary and curable. Once an acute illness is cured, it is gone. It doesn't leave behind lasting physical damage that might weaken you.

A good example of an acute condition is appendicitis. The doctor treats the condition by operating and removing the infected appendix, which, fortunately, is an organ the body doesn't need. People usually recover from the operation (doctors call it an *appendectomy*) within a period of weeks and go back to their normal activities. People who have had an appendectomy don't have to go through a long period of rehabilitation or monitoring unless there are complications.

Other types of acute problems include:

• flu
• earaches

- sore throats
- minor surgery

Chronic illnesses, on the other hand, are diseases or conditions that do not have a short-term cure. Many have no cure at all, though most can be treated in a way that helps the person live more comfortably and sometimes more vigorously than with no treatment at all.

While chronic diseases are treatable, they are also permanent and irreversible. A patient with a chronic disease needs training to learn to "manage" the disease—that is, to live with it as comfortably as possible. Such a patient may also need to be monitored or medically supervised for a long period of time. In some cases the patient may need rehabilitation in order to get back to near normal functioning. Often, the best one can hope for is a lessened degree of disability.

Chronic disease can be emotionally and spiritually difficult for both patients and loved ones. Persons who can't get about much find their lives severely narrowing. Sometimes that narrowing means a break-down of mental functions, simply because they aren't getting practice. Learning to live a relatively confined life can also be very trying emotionally. For the family, too, there is the pain of watching a dear one weaken and pine.

Chronic illness requires management by household members and patients as well. Often patients require continued monitoring, or rehabilitation or other kinds of long-term care services. Patients may also have to take several medications to help manage pain or control symptoms and complication. All in all, such disease can put a great strain on the household.

As the lists make clear, not all chronic problems are caused by disease. Conditions like stroke or disfigurement obviously create long-term problems. People with these conditions may not feel sick, but the effects can still be devastating.

PREVENTION OF CHRONIC DISEASE

Some chronic diseases and conditions are preventable. Let's use osteoporosis as our example. Osteoporosis results when the bones lose minerals and become brittle. It affects over twenty-five million

SOME CHARACTERISTICS OF CHRONIC ILLNESSES

The condition is permanent

The condition is irreversible

The patient must have special training to learn to manage the illness

The patient may need to be monitored or supervised for a long period of time.

The patient may need rehabilitation to reach maximal functioning.

The illness can be associated with varying degrees of disability.

The entire family is affected by the psychosocial implications of long-term health problems.

The patient must make emotional adjustment to the condition.

SOME COMMON CHRONIC DISEASES

Here is a list of some common chronic diseases.

Diabetes	Muscular Dystrophy
Arthritis	Cerebral Palsy
Osteoporosis	Myasthenia Gravis
Alzheimer's Disease	Parkinson's disease
AIDS	Schizophrenia
Multiple Sclerosis	Chronic Obstructive Pulmonary Disease (COPD)
ALS (Lou Gehrig's Disease)	Some Types of Cancer

SOME CHRONIC HEALTH CONDITIONS

Take some time with the congregational members on your team to think about and discuss the conditions listed below to see what these conditions have in common with each other and with the illnesses listed above. By doing that, you will come to a solid understanding of chronic illness.

Birth Defects and Birthmarks

Other Types of Disfigurement

Spinal Cord Injury

Head Injury

Amputation

Stroke

Down Syndrome

Severe Burns

Colostomy (bowel movements are collected outside the body through an opening in the abdomen instead of the usual way, usually due to cancer)

Mastectomy (removal of a breast, usually due to cancer)

Some Types of Cancer

Americans, eighty-five percent of them women. This disease tends to occur in older people and, if bones are broken, a serious handicap or even the inability to walk around can result.

Congregational health programs can help prevent this disease by organizing informative programs to teach people how to reduce the risk and strengthen bones at an early age. (See the section on "Osteoporosis" in Chapter 3.) People who *aren't* young can help themselves through mineral supplements and exercise. They need to see their doctors to work out healthy bone programs for themselves and their families. By sharing information, congregational members can agree on which doctors are best able and ready to give this kind of help.

Osteoporosis provides an easy example of how the congregation can work powerful changes in the health awareness of its members. The more we understand about our own health, the more likely we are to enjoy good health.

A secondary benefit is that the congregation will experience how the power of an idea can set positive change in motion. Then they'll know the rewards of working for one's community—both the community at hand and the community of our grandchildren, who may enjoy the blessing of being born into a community that cares about each member's health.

HOW THE CONGREGATION CAN HELP

Congregations can help prevent the development of certain chronic illnesses and conditions and can also give loving kindness to those who suffer from such diseases and conditions in any number of ways. For example, a person who has just been diagnosed with a chronic illness or who suffers from the after-effects of one will experience emotional anguish. A stroke can set in motion long bouts of depression. Parkinson's disease and multiple sclerosis can trigger deep, long-lasting sorrow in those who struggle to cope with a series of losses as the disease progresses.

We've spoken of these struggles in psychological terms, but they are also spiritual struggles. Even a strong faith may be called into question. Some people may think that they are being punished, and others may find themselves furious with a God that can allow them to suffer.

The role of the congregation is to offer comfort by helping the afflicted person cultivate in the patient states of mind that can be positive and beneficial. Such states of mind are called "coping strategies"—which are simply strategies that allow a person to live more comfortably with problems he or she can't change. But before we introduce you to effective coping strategies, here's a bit more you must know about living with chronic illness.

PHYSICAL CHANGES IN CHRONIC ILLNESS

Helping others with chronic illness requires that you understand the illness well enough to put yourself in their shoes. Although each case is different, all people with chronic illness are likely to experience one or even all the following:

- pain
- decreased ability to perform daily tasks
- need for medications or other treatment to help manage symptoms

Pain

Pain may range from mild to severe, and it can vary from day to day and from person to person. People often simply learn to live with it. Older people who live with pain often learn to tolerate it, by necessity. They know that it's just part of getting old.

Whether pain is tolerable or intolerable isn't something that can be measured from the outside. Be guided by the saying, common in the health profession, that "pain is whatever the person says it is." You're not helping people who hurt by telling them that they don't really hurt.

When people tell you they have excruciating pain, you must believe them, even if you think they look fine. Then you'll find it easy to provide empathy and understanding. Remember too that for people to express their pain or discomfort and get kindness and understanding back can sometimes ease the pain.

Disability

Chronic illness can cause deterioration of the body, loss of strength, and even progressive inability to control the body. Weakness or pain can make carrying out simple jobs—such as getting dressed, feeding oneself, or bathing (called "activities of daily living" or ADLs)—increasingly difficult. A person may need help to perform basic tasks, such as managing bowel and bladder functions.

In all these matters, loss of independence creates a cascade of emotions that can turn out to be an additional burden. Anger and sadness can become overwhelming to a person who must go through such losses without support.

THE ELDERLY

Even older people who have always lived organized and effective lives will eventually find themselves unable to do things they've always done. Such things (ADLs) may include:

- housekeeping
- cooking
- driving
- balancing the checkbook
- grocery shopping
- walking and exercising
- talking on the phone

Congregational members can organize groups of people who are especially interested in helping with one or another of these ADLs.

Transportation

Transportation is often a problem for older people and for people with disabilities. They may need help just to get to doctors' appointments or therapy. Even surgery from which a healthy person usually recovers quite well (hip replacement or cataracts, for example) can restrict driving for a while. City transportation often does not accommodate people in wheelchairs. Rural communities usually don't offer public transportation. Both in cities and in the country, people may find that they can't get to worship services just because they have nobody to drive them.

For all these reasons, *a transportation ministry can be a strong outreach of the congregation.*

Stroke

A stroke can leave a person with serious physical losses like:

- inability to speak or eat
- paralysis of one side of the body
- chronic fatigue

Further, the person's outward appearance changes, as when one half of the face becomes paralyzed. He or she may feel stared at, and as a result may limit social activities and withdraw more and more from others.

Support groups help stroke survivors and their families deal with loss. Consider starting a stroke support group in your own church if that can help meet the needs of your congregation or larger community. That group can help the person learn to use the coping strategies we discuss below.

Amputation

A person whose leg has been amputated may have to learn how to walk again with an artificial leg, or may have to use a wheelchair. To make matters worse, amputees may experience phantom limb pain (painful sensations that make it feel like the missing limb is still there).

Here, once again, the congregation can lend emotional support. People of faith need to love those who are different from themselves as much as they love themselves.

The church has historically been noted for caring attitudes and a strong sense of community well-being. And don't forget the practical side of caring: *Be sure that your buildings are accessible and welcoming to all who wish to enter, including those who are in some way disabled.*

EMOTIONAL EFFECTS OF CHRONIC ILLNESS

People with chronic health problems may experience loss and grief, denial, anger, sorrow, guilt, and self-blame. The high cost of long-term health care or repeated hospitalization may cause economic difficulties. Money problems obviously can also feed depression. Indeed, given the combination of strains that can result from chronic health problems, both individuals and families may feel that God has abandoned them.

A person who has spent his or her life doing charitable deeds may feel cheated when they find themselves "punished" instead of rewarded.

Diseases like HIV/AIDS, which can develop into chronic conditions, present special problems. HIV/AIDS takes many innocent victims, but because it is also associated with homosexual activity or drug abuse, the victim may also feel condemned by the community, and even self-condemned.

In some cases, out of dread of the judgment of others, a person may keep the diagnosis a secret for as long as possible—even from fellow members of the congregation. Such hiding adds still another layer to what the person is suffering already. It also can delay treatment and, in some cases, spread the disease to others.

We think the congregation does best by discussing such matters openly in organized groups. Otherwise, guilt can spread through the congregation like an epidemic.

An excellent book on how congregations can learn to talk about subjects that have always been taboo is Geneveva E. Belle's *My Rose: An African American Mother's Story of AIDS*. At the end of each chapter there are study questions designed to guide congregational study group.

Guilt

A person who has smoked cigarettes for years and now is diagnosed with lung cancer may feel guilt and sorrow that his or her actions led to this problem. Other people may make the person feel still worse by making negative comments, like, "Well, you brought it on yourself." While the congregation should certainly organize educational programs on the many very real dangers of smoking, little good can be served by condemning someone who already suffers, whatever the cause.

Remember that to view illness as a punishment from God places a heavy burden on people to live a perfectly pure life. People who feel guilty because they can't come up to such standards, and who see sickness as punishment, will naturally experience spiritual distress. *Such feelings should be discussed within the faith community.*

COPING WITH CHRONIC CONDITIONS

How we "cope" is how we deal with a situation—especially, an unfavorable situation. There can be negative as well as positive forms of coping. Getting drunk, getting high on drugs, or having promiscuous sex may be ways of coping, but in the long run they don't work, since they bring their own stress and anxiety, and too often end in addiction and even prison.

People who use negative coping strategies in response to chronic illness often create additional devastating consequences, because rather than learning to adjust to their condition, they remain in a state of denial, avoidance, or anger.

A long list of positive coping strategies will include good diet and good rest, exercise, and visits from caring people that give patients a feeling of human presence and community. For many, prayer and meditation also serve well.

A positive coping strategy is one that keeps people feeling positive even in the midst of distress. Such strategies, which a person must cultivate inwardly, include:

- prayer and scripture reading
- humor
- a sense of control
- positive thinking

Prayer

People of faith have always turned to prayer as a means of coping in times of trouble. The Psalms are King David's prayers that he cried out to God in moments of great trial. "Pray without ceasing," Paul wrote in a letter to one early church (1 Thessalonians 4:17). Similarly today, spiritual leaders encourage us to pray for mercy and strength during our own times of trouble. Christians, Muslims,

Jews, and followers of many other faiths believe that regular prayer and meditation strengthen the spiritual self and bring eventual peace, no matter how hard the circumstances.

Some physicians incorporate prayer as part of their practice, praying with their patients prior to surgery. Nurses are sometimes called upon to pray for or with a patient for whom they are caring. Encourage those who are comfortable with the practice to find comfort from disease in prayer.

It may be helpful to organize a group from your church who will pray regularly with people in need. But keep in mind that some people are private with their prayer life and would prefer that others pray *for* them throughout the week. Find out what feels most comfortable for the person and plan from there.

Scripture Reading

Several of the major faiths see the Bible as divinely inspired. For believers, to read scripture is to hear the words of the Heavenly Father Himself comforting us directly.

In Chapter 3, we listed scripture references that can help people face particular health problems. Those who wish to minister comfort to people with chronic illness can write Bible verses on a card as a spiritual gift, or can read the verses to the person who needs comfort. Even reading them over the phone can help.

Some sections of the Bible may be more helpful than others in encouraging people who suffer. During times of crisis and physical suffering, people often turn to the *Psalms* for comfort. *Proverbs* contains wisdom and advice. *Job* teaches the lessons of long-suffering faith. *Isaiah* 53 looks toward the suffering and humility suffered by the Messiah Himself. Christians who physically suffer will sometimes gain comfort from the story of the crucifixion as it recounts how Jesus suffered great physical pain for their sins. Such Christians can identify their own pain with the afflictions He experienced as a man.

When you first use Scripture to provide comfort to people with chronic problems, ask if they have used the Bible in this way before. Even if they haven't, it may be appropriate to suggest to people of faith that Bible passages can be an additional source of strength that has worked for others in similar situations. If the person has favorite passages, offer to write these out and place them where he or she can read them daily.

Some people are most encouraged by the direct teachings of Christ, so a red-letter Bible that highlights Jesus' words would be a good gift to them. It is not uncommon for people who have previously stopped reading their Bibles to return to the Scriptures for comfort in times of trouble.

ORGANIZING SERVICES FOR PEOPLE WITH CHRONIC ILLNESS

Faith communities are noted for providing help, care, and service to people in need. Here are some guidelines for organizing such service for people with chronic illness.

It couldn't be simpler. First, identify those people in your congregation who have long-term care needs, are hurting, or grieving, or ill. Second, organize groups of people who wish to serve them.

Because women tend to outlive men, as your congregation ages, there are likely to be many widows who need some extra care and attention. Visits from the pastors are always welcome, but they do not replace the continued, planned care that a group of people dedicated to this type of ministry can provide.

We emphasize that help should be continuous. It is all too easy to provide strong support when a devastating injury first happens or that dreaded diagnosis is made. But sometimes, as time goes on, the person with continued problems is forgotten and, along with the family, feels abandoned.

Support of the faith community can take many forms. Preparing and delivering meals can sometimes be helpful, just as it is for people with temporary problems, like recovering from surgery or having a baby. But those who suffer from chronic problems may also require a continuing plan:

- Homebound people will welcome visits, which can be planned.
- People unable to attend worship services will also welcome

bulletins and tapes of the service, which can be mailed to them and keep them connected.
- Phone calls are an easy way to show people that you care.
- Youth in the church can help do household chores or outdoor cleanup at the person's home.

In all these ways and more the faith community can show support for the person with long-term health problems.

Humor

More and more evidence suggests that humor can relieve stress and even help heal. Norman Cousins, a pioneer in this field, found that watching old Marx brothers movies and reruns of Sid Caesar's *Show of Shows* made him laugh, and that laughter was a relief from severe pain caused by a cancer from which doctors didn't give him much chance of recovering. Cousins, at least, believed that his laughter was a key part of his cure.

Even doctors have been persuaded. Some, including Patch Adams and Neil Shulman ("Doc Hollywood")—both of them of movie fame—have made laughter part of the prescription. See their web sites, which are rich resources:

www.patchadams.com/media.html
www.patientcommunications.com

Some congregations may find humor inappropriate for a church. If so, what follows in this section isn't for them. But we think that humor can be an important part of the larger ministry. Here are some ways we've found to work, and you'll come up with more of your own:

- Include books, tapes, and videos of notable comedians of your faith in your library or church book center.
- Have a cartoon board in the bathroom facilities. Members can submit cartoons to a committee to screen them for appropriateness.
- Some churches bring in clown groups to teach young people to be professional clowns, so that young people can visit hospitals

and nursing homes, where there is a great need for laughter.
Young clowns can also paint faces and make animal balloons at
church picnics and community fairs.
* Puppets provide another way for incorporating humor into a
  variety of settings and for many age groups. There are training
  workshops and seminars to learn these arts, and associations
  that support them are springing up in major cities everywhere.
* You might want to bring on the clowns.

All you need to begin such a ministry is a couple of adults willing to learn these techniques and then teach them to others.

Control

People find comfort in feeling they have some control over their situations. People who are ill may also try to keep that control as a way
of coping. Sometimes that may come across as being pretty stub-
born or ill-tempered, and other people may see them as grumpy,
irritable, or bossy.

Before you take on the task of soothing and encouraging such
people, consider that they have experienced so extreme a loss that
they have lost control of their lives. Understand that at times they
may have even more trouble remaining sweet-tempered than the
rest of us.

Help them to restore some sense of control by offering choices.
True, in some cases, like diet, there might not be much choice. With
high blood pressure, for example, it's best to stay away from salt; if
cholesterol is high, it's best to stay away from too much fat and oil.
(In fact, even if blood pressure and cholesterol are fine, it's better to
stay away from too much salt, fat,and oil.)

Restrictions placed on a person by chronic illness can of course
go far beyond not being able to eat all the salt and grease he or she
wants. But no matter how serious the situation, some choice
remains, and small choices can add a lot to the quality of life. Just
deciding what to wear or when to take a shower can help foster a
sense of control. So, even, can choosing to change the channel, or
listening to a special piece of music, or enjoying the company of a
special person.

Find ways to nurture and enforce this powerful coping strategy. *Do what you can to offer the person you serve some choices.* For many people who suffer, having choices is the beginning of a tranquility that comes from knowing how to live with what can't change.

Positive Thinking

After extreme loss, people can fall into black moods, dwelling on what they've lost and on the diminished life that remains. We don't mean to say that people who have gone through such loss shouldn't have such thoughts and feelings. They have every right to grieve over their loss. But healing grief, though it may never end, entails getting on with other things. In their own time, the bereaved will return to living and appreciate the precious moments that life gives to those ready to take them.

People with chronic illness can get locked into depression, as if mourning for themselves. The congregation must use discretion here, by allowing people their grief, but, at the same time, working to bring cheer to people who have suffered loss of health.

Besides the strategies we've already talked about, consider other ways of bringing cheer:

- Visits for an hour each week, to comfort the patient and restore his or her sense of connection to the outside world
- Phone calls
- Helping the person write cards and letters
- Christmas caroling at the door

Special projects will occur to you, according to the customs of your congregation. A Sunday school class might purchase an inspirational book for the patient. Magazine subscriptions can help. For example, *Guideposts* is an inexpensive, monthly, nondenominational magazine written in easy-to-read format that emphasizes positive thinking through the telling of true stories. Seek out specific ways to promote positive thinking in those who use this as a coping mechanism. Remember to emphasize the positive in each situation.

Hope and Faith

For people who embrace Judeo-Christian values, hope is an essential foundation of faith. Hebrews 11:1 tells us that ". . . faith is the substance of things hoped for, the evidence of things not seen." People who live with the knowledge and experience of a higher power have reason to hope. To them, life is more than the material play of things we see here on earth. Some people experience all existence as the garment of God. Other people have hope for a better hereafter, or at least freedom from the oppressions and illnesses of the present world. Some version of this faith is the promise of the world's religions.

Nurses often hear people with chronic health problems say that what keeps them going is hope for a cure, or even, simply, hope that they will feel a little better. The fact is that new cures *are* discovered. While there is life there is hope. The alternative to hope is depression, fear, and anxiety, and if these were on the menu, few of us would order them.

We think there is always room for hope and faith. Sometimes a situation looks so bleak that medical professionals say, "There is no hope." But hope and faith have a way of staying alive in certain strong hearts, even though they may appear to be extinguished. We've known people who, while doctors gave them up for lost, did not give themselves up. Some of them made good recoveries. We believe there is always room for hope, there is always room for faith. Even today, faith can sometimes move mountains.

Don't give false hope, but as long as the person who is ill has hope, don't try to take it away. If there is still some harsh lesson to be learned, circumstance will soon enough ease the person into that recognition. So foster hope and encourage faith. Wise men know that difficult times do pass and we cannot be sure what the future will hold.

Presence

Perhaps the most wonderful gift you can give to a person with a chronic illness is the gift of your physical presence. Sending cards and making phone calls are good things to do, and are also very easy. Being there on a regular basis and in times of crisis is more challenging and more rewarding. Loneliness is common among older people, in part because they often have difficulty getting out of the house. But for people with health problems, the isolation can be even worse. For a person with chronic lung problems, for instance, the effort of carrying along an oxygen tank in order to get out of the house may just not be worth it.

You'll find people happy to make sure no one in the congregation, or even in the larger immediate community, is without the comfort of visits. The coordinator of your congregational health program can establish a visitation program for people at home or in nursing homes, simply by organizing a group of volunteers. The director of nursing or social worker for the nursing home can provide a list of residents who would most benefit from such visits.

Exercise

For anyone able to move at all, exercise at any level brings great benefits, both physical and emotional. Among those benefits, exercise

- improves circulation and mobility
- helps relieve stress
- reduces pain
- fosters a sense of well being
- promotes a sense of having more control

For people in moderately good health, exercise can mean biking, swimming, jogging, working out in a gym, or simply walking for half an hour each day. But even those who are bedridden can lift light weights or do other simple exercises from a wheelchair—*and* enjoy the benefits!

Exercises for People with Chronic Conditions

- People with arthritis often find aquatics helpful. The water provides resistive exercise and at the same time makes exercise less painful by cushioning and supporting the joints.
- Stationary bicycles and treadmills are good for people with adequate balance and stability. Treadmills should have bars to hold onto for safety. Stationary bikes are good for those people who would be unable to balance on a regular bike outside, but

stationary bicycles mainly work the lower extremities, and thus provide less of an aerobic or cardiovascular workout than walking does.

- Weight training, usually at a gym, is one of the newest techniques for building strength and endurance, even among the disabled and/or elderly.
- Walking is one of the best overall exercises for the older adult, or for people with chronic health problems. Regular walking can decrease stress, promote a positive sense of well-being, and improve the cardiovascular system. Along with dietary changes, walking is also a good way to lose weight.

Even for those who are bedbound (in bed most of the time) exercises can bring benefits. Here are some suggestions:

1. For people able to use it, install a trapeze over the bed. This device not only helps with bed mobility (turning and positioning), but it also helps strengthen the arms and upper body.

2. Leg lifts (unless the physician or therapist says not to do this) can be done in bed. Space out the exercises: try to start with ten repetitions twice a day, then three times per day for maybe a week. In the second week do fifteen repetitions three times per day, and gradually work up to more.

3. The patient should try to find a comfortable exercise for each major muscle group. For example: *Arm raises:* Regular use of even light weights –three pounds might be good—in bed helps strengthen the arms. *Leg lifts, knee bends, shoulder shrugs, rotating the ankles, turning the head from side to side*—all work to stretch the joints and stretch the muscles. Even *turning side to side in bed* works some muscles. The patient should rest between exercises as necessary.

A physical therapist can help devise an exercise plan for each patient before discharge from the hospital to a home setting. That plan will be unique to each person, depending on the diagnosis and the extent of physical illness or disability.

The main rule of thumb is that *a person should do as much as possible for him or herself.* "A joint that moves is a joint that functions," so any exercise is better than none.

People with breathing difficulties often find it hard to walk any distance. But remember that even older people can accumulate the effects of exercise. The person should start walking for just a few minutes each day. If the person keeps it up, he or she will become stronger and have more stamina for longer walks.

In the case of people who can't exercise in bed because they are too weak, paralyzed, or immobile, family members can help by moving their joints to help keep them from getting stiff and contracted.

If people do *not* move their joints in some way but just lie in bed, their bodies will tend to curl up. This is because the muscles that contract are stronger than the ones that extend. All joints must be moved, and muscles need to be used so that they do not shrivel and waste away. It is essential that if people do not bear weight or stand on their own, other people help them maintain some type of mobility. Always stretch those fingers, arms, and legs to their full extension.

Here is a real life example. Donna was an obese forty-two-year-old woman with a history of severe asthma. She was told she needed to lose weight, but she could barely walk down the street without getting very short of breath.

Through prayer and by committing this need to God, Donna began daily morning walks. First she went for only five minutes and then had to return home, barely making it to the end of the road. But she continued to pray for strength and she continued to do her five minutes per day, and this quickly paid off.

The second week she was able to go a little farther, and the next week, a little farther still. After a year of prayer and dedication to eating right and walking, Donna lost over eighty pounds and was able to walk at a quick pace for several miles. She looked healthier and felt better. She thanked God for helping her through the tough early going. Even her asthma was much better after her lifestyle changes.

The rule of thumb is that any activity is better than none. Old people and people who aren't feeling too well may at first show resistance. (Younger people often show it, too, fearing that the long-term commitment will be too demanding.) There's always an excuse for *not* starting to exercise.

But getting started is the key, so your job is to reassure people in advance that they will not be asked to do more than they can. Each person will set his or her own agenda, and the only challenge will be reaching his or her own goals. Let the person suggest activities he or she would like to do—maybe it's an assisted walk, maybe some work with light weights, under supervision. If the person doesn't come up with anything, you can make a suggestion.

Remember that people with chronic health problems have to alternate between rest and activity. Be alert that they may tire easily. Gradually, together, you will have a clear notion of what's enough and what's too much.

Besides helping people to exercise, you might want to assist a local nursing home or adult foster home with walking the residents. Keeping older people up and walking is one of the most essential tasks in preventing immobility and further disease, and in promoting health. Many such nursing and foster homes welcome outside assistance. And it goes without saying that the people who live there will welcome it, too.

PROPER NUTRITION

Eating right means eating a variety of healthy foods. Eating right helps the body heal. But eating right can be a problem for the ill. They may not have much appetite because of symptoms of their diseases or because of side effects from their medicines. Or, once home, they may have appetite, but feel too tired to fix a nutritional meal.

Programs such as Meals on Wheels are helpful in such cases, but congregational members can also assist. Some congregations prepare a week of meals ahead of time and put them in the freezer of the person they're caring for.

If you decide to undertake a ministry in this area, be sure to check the dietary restrictions or special needs of each patient. Many people with chronic illnesses are on special diets involving, for example, high amounts of vitamins and protein for healing, or restricted salt or fat. People on such diets will usually have a written list of allowable foods that can be used to help plan meals. Encouraging fluid intake is especially important among the elderly (unless restricted by their physician) as a way to prevent dehydration that can lead to other health problems.

REST

Even without special health problems, older people often don't sleep as long or as well as they did when they were younger. People with chronic illnesses or disease, especially, may not get good rest because of pain, coughing, or simple insomnia. Insomnia is a frequent complaint of older adults and at present there's no recommended cure for it.

There are, however, some things you can do to make it more likely that the people you are helping get good rest:

- Help people decide which does them more good: napping during the day or sleeping better at night. Taking naps during the day can make it more difficult to sleep at night.
- Help them to determine whether any particular fears or worries keep them awake, and also, what thoughts, or images, or music help them sleep better. Encourage them to focus on a pleasant memory or image as they prepare for sleep.
- Encourage them to explore the things that help them rest. Sometimes, whatever our ages, there are facts we still need to learn for ourselves—like what helps us fall asleep.

SUMMARY

People with chronic illness, disease, or other long-term conditions experience a lot of physical and emotional stress. They deal with this stress in ways that can be positive or negative. The faith community, particularly through congregational health programs, is in a unique position to minister to its own members and to the larger community by helping foster positive coping strategies. Discuss the suggestions offered in this chapter and decide how your church can best help people with long-term problems.

REFERENCE

Belle, Geneveva E.: *My Rose: An African American Mother's Story of AIDS.* Pilgrim Press, 1997.

NINE

DEALING WITH CRISIS AND LOSS

Sometimes life does not seem fair, and we can never know when such times might come. No one is immune from crisis or the experience of grief. Indeed, these very experiences draw people to the church, where they seek meaning or peace during times of distress.

This chapter offers ways that communities of faith can provide assistance to people who are in crisis or who are grieving.

UNDERSTANDING AND COPING WITH CRISES

Crises are human experiences caused by a stressful event or the perception of threat, and they are a natural part of our human existence. Crises usually mean some kind of bad news, ranging from mishaps to deaths of loved ones. As the world grows more dangerous, crises are also linked to our experience of world events.

Whatever triggers a crisis, the response can be overwhelming. Our ordinary ways of coping no longer work, as we slowly and painfully learn to adjust to a world that's been changed and diminished for us by loss.

It's natural that a terrible sense of loss often accompanies a feeling of crisis. So if you want to help someone in crisis, you must have a keen understanding of what they are going through. Only then can

CRISES AND THEIR SYMPTOMS

Crises are very closely associated with a large number of physical and emotional complaints. You need to be able to recognize them.

Physical Complaints:

Headaches   Gastrointestinal upset

Backaches   No interest in sex

Sleep disturbances   Difficulty sleeping

Sleeping all the time   Nightmares

Other Changes Brought on by Crisis:

Emotional expressions (anger, crying, sadness, guilt, apathy)

Intellectual changes (difficulty concentrating, forgetfulness)

Social withdrawal

Spiritual distress (helplessness, hopelessness, suicidal thoughts)

you begin to bring them toward the strong healing that is often rooted in crisis.

At the moment of sudden loss, people react in different ways. Some get through such crises unaided. The problem eases, they receive support from others, or they find support in strategies that have helped them in the past. Recovery needs a kind of faith, essentially spiritual, that their lives are livable—which is to say, worth living. Some people have that faith at all times, maybe more when it is most tested.

But others in crisis will experience great anxiety and stress. They've been handed a situation they've never had to face before. All their usual ways of grappling with problems are stymied. This one's too big, the threat or sense of loss too great. People in crisis can feel that they have lost control of their lives.

It is right here, in the heart of the trouble, that many people discover an opportunity that can patiently be made from the loss. It is here that they learn new ways of coping.

Grief is a natural process, the universal response to loss. It is a powerful experience that affects people physically, emotionally, socially, and spiritually. The ability to experience grief is linked to our ability to form meaningful relationships. It is because we have loved that we grieve.

Often our grief is associated with the death of a loved one, and this is one of the deepest forms of loss. John (11: 34) tells us that even Jesus wept when he learned of his friend Lazarus' death. But grief can also occur in response to the loss of a job, dream, ideal, pet, or valuable object. We must simply keep in mind that for the person who grieves the sense of loss is real and terrible.

COMMON RESPONSES TO GRIEF

Nothing can be more individual than grief, but, as you saw in the last section, there are certain common responses to grief that can affect:

- how we feel physically and emotionally
- the way we think
- the strength of our spiritual lives

Here's a chart that will help you see specific ways that grief can be expressed by a person. While grief is not the same as depression, it can become depression if the grief reaction does not follow its usual course and allow the person to work through the loss.

HOW A PERSON MAY EXPRESS GRIEF

Physical
Crying
Low energy
Shortness of breath
Sleep changes
Tightness in chest
Muscle weakness
Stomach upset
Appetite changes

Emotional
Sadness
Anger
Anxiety
Relief
Guilt
Irritability
Euphoria
Fear
Numbness
Loneliness

Cognitive
Disbelief
Confusion
Hallucinations
Obsessive thoughts
Forgetfulness
Panic

Spiritual
Alienation
Hopelessness

THE FOUR TASKS OF GRIEVING

Bereavement expert J. William Worden identifies four tasks associated with the work of grieving in his book, *Grief Counseling & Grief Therapy: A Guide for the Mental Health Professional.*

Task One is to accept the reality of the loss. You may have experienced that state in which something so bad has happened that you want to think that it was a bad dream—*anything* to make it seem less real, less threatening. That's what people can feel when they experience the death of a loved one or a bad diagnosis or the loss of a job.

Accepting the reality of the loss is especially difficult when the loss is sudden, such as the death of a spouse in an automobile accident. It is easier to say, "this cannot be true" than to acknowledge that the person is never coming home again. So the first hard task the griever must accept is the fact of the loss.

Task Two is to experience the pain of grief. There is no avoiding the pain of grief. Grief is our way of honoring what we have lost, whether it be a person who died or a long-held dream. Each person progresses through this pain at his or her own pace, but it is a pain that has to be experienced, not numbed. Medications or other substances that might numb the feelings of grief are not usually recommended for the mourner.

Task Three is to adjust to an environment in which the deceased is missing. Once a person has done the grieving, in whatever time it takes, he or she must turn to the task of constructing a new life. The loss of a spouse changes not only the big things but the small things as well. It changes how we live our lives.

When people have been together for a long time, they support each other in any number of ways. Maybe a man has to learn to prepare his own meals and balance the checkbook for the first time. Maybe a woman has to get a job, or make decisions her husband used to make.

Losing a spouse is hard. Losing a child can be even harder. For the grieving parent, the question "Why?" may often ring loud. So, too, the daily ache of the child's absence. In addition, there can be the specific pains of particular situations.

Consider the mother who has managed the care of her chronically ill child. When the child dies, the mother must go on living in a world no longer defined by blood tests, physician appointments, medications. It's as if she must invent a whole new sense of the normal, the ordinary, from which her child has been withdrawn.

We can't expect people to perform the task of healing from such a loss hurriedly. It can be months or longer before the mourner is ready to begin to move on and make the new arrangements—emotional, practical, and spiritual—that life now requires.

Task Four is to withdraw emotional energy from grieving and to reinvest it in other activities. Eventually, most people get through task three and rearrange the practical aspects of their lives as required. But there remains another phase of the healing. To a person in acute grief, it may seem, paradoxically, that all human contact is impossible except contact with the person who is lost. Now the aim must be not to forget the dead but to move beyond the emotional chains of maintaining a one-sided relationship by reconnecting with the living.

Slowly, grievers will begin again to take care of themselves and to take care of others. They may take up new hobbies or interests, engage in new relationships. Slowly, they return to a new sense of normalcy. That normalcy may include a shadow of sadness but it also offers occasions for renewal and joy.

In his book, J. William Worden describes what the grief counselor works to accomplish:

- To help the survivor actualize the loss
- To help the survivor to identify and express feelings
- To assist the survivor in living without the deceased
- To provide time for grief and know how to interpret its symptoms as "normal" behavior
- To allow for individual differences
- To provide for continued support
- To examine defenses and coping styles
- To identify serious, and potentially dangerous, depression and refer it to the proper health care agency
- To help free up the survivor's emotions from preoccupation with the deceased

These tasks are difficult, but remember that, at the most basic level, you help the mourner simply by being available. The church has traditionally taken on this role and it is often anticipated and accepted by the grieving family.

As you work to help a person with grieving and healing, learn to listen without offering advice. This kind of listening can be difficult because it is natural to want to try to make things better, but it can be learned. Sometimes, the only way "to make things better" is to let the person voice grief.

Specific scriptural readings to comfort the bereaved can be helpful. Prayer can also be a great support. Timing is important here. Be aware that the bereaved may hold a great deal of anger, with some of this anger directed at God; understand that this is normal and even emotionally natural. Once the grief can find expression, it usually passes with time.

In assisting the bereaved, you will need to be patient. There is no set length of time for mourning. Some people take months, others require years to complete the work of grieving. That is why you must make yourself available to the bereaved for as long as you are needed. In the early days following the loss, the person is often surrounded by friends and family. As the weeks and months pass and other people have returned to their routines, you can play a critical role in remembering the mourner and continue to come to his or her side.

Special holidays or anniversaries can be especially difficult for people who have experienced loss. Let them know that you remember them (and their loved ones) during these difficult days.

Through your health ministry, your congregation can offer support groups for people who have experienced loss. You may wish to provide groups that target specific types of loss such as divorce or death of a spouse or child. In addition to providing members of the group with a safe place to share their feelings and experiences, you can offer them the means to establish new and meaningful relationships through the group.

RESOLVING CRISES

Although a crisis can have devastating effects, it *can* be resolved when a person learns to use new coping strategies that let him or her gradually *redefine the event or threat in such a way that the spiritual opportunities offered by the crisis can be recognized and experienced.*

Most periods of individual crisis resolve in six to eight weeks, often with the person functioning at the same level as before. Indeed, some people come through this situation feeling that they are stronger because of the crisis.

But while many people *do* recover quickly, others spiral into a state of serious disequilibrium and require professional psychiatric care.

MATURATIONAL CRISES

Health professionals speak of two types of crises: *maturational* and *situational*. Maturational crises are associated with transitional periods when we make role shifts. They occur at every stage of life. They include such crossings as the child becoming a man, the man and the woman becoming a couple, or any human being wrestling with aging, sickness, or even dying.

EXAMPLES OF MATURATIONAL AND SITUATIONAL CRISES

Maturational	Situational
Middle Childhood	Divorce
Adolescence	Sexual Assault
Attending College Away from Home	Death of a Loved One
	Diagnosis of a Chronic Illness
Marriage	Unwanted Pregnancy
Parenthood	School Difficulties
Midlife	Household Fire
Retirement	Natural disasters
	Terrorist Activity

Retirement is a time when many people experience a maturational crisis. Consider Sam, who is sixty-five years old and has worked at the same factory for fifty years. Every morning for fifty years, before his shift, Sam would meet his work friends for coffee and a sweet roll at the bakery next to the company. For Sam, this breakfast crowd was a community rich with laughs and shared wisdom.

Sam never had had to worry much about recreation. He put in long hard days and usually did not have energy even to think about activities that might tickle his interests. Work took it out of Sam, but he liked it. In a way, work was a like church, something to go to regularly. Sam *did* attend church regularly on Sundays, often serving as an usher for the early service.

When Sam retired, he did not know what to do with all his free time. He missed the company of his work friends and he didn't have any hobbies or interests to keep him active. Sam had a hard time.

For a while Sam kept going to church. But about a month after he retired, Sam began to feel anxious. He stayed in bed most days, lost some weight, and didn't sleep well. Sam also eventually stopped attending church, which was a kind of last step toward nearly complete social withdrawal.

The crisis that Sam experienced after his retirement happened because Sam wasn't prepared for his major life transition. It is a sad example of a maturational crisis.

SITUATIONAL CRISES

Situational crises occur when a specific life event upsets a person's balance. You'll find examples on the list and in your memory. Crises are part of our common experience, after all, even though they can hit us all differently.

What Jenny went through during and after her divorce is a good example. Jenny and Matt married seven years ago—say, in your church. To most of their friends, theirs seemed to be a dream marriage: they had three beautiful children, a house in the country, and Matt's start-up business was taking off in a big way.

When Matt asked for a divorce, Jenny hadn't seen it coming. She'd looked forward to raising the children with her husband, and she sometimes looked even past that to their golden years. She loved Matt. Now she had to deal with the loss of this dream, the breakup of their home and business, and shared custody of the children.

It wasn't a friendly divorce. Even meeting in church on Sunday was too painful. Jenny eventually found another church.

Jenny had never felt so low. Her usual coping strategies, and her talent for fixing problems as soon as they came up, just didn't work. She'd always enjoyed the comfort of talking things over with Matt, so that when they faced a problem, they faced it together. Now she found it painful to face life alone.

For a while Jenny continued to pray and exercise, which had always been key coping strategies for her. But they no longer worked, and after a while her exercise fell off, then her prayers. For Jenny, divorce was a situational crisis. She had reached a point where she just didn't know how to go on with her life.

Not all situational crises are personal. *Situational crises can also occur to individuals or groups of people who experience sudden and unexpected changes in their lives as the result of natural disasters, accidents, or acts of violence.* Events such as tornadoes, fires, earthquakes, hurricanes, or floods are situational crises that can affect whole communities. We find it difficult even to speak of the disasters of September 11th. These disasters are so great that we can't shut them out, the way we shut out distant troubles or catastrophes. And, every day, it seems our lives are so rocked by these huge disasters and our own anxiety that, in the language of Job, God no longer puts a hedge around us.

At home, too, our lives can be touched by violent disasters— school shootings, mass kidnappings, airplane crashes, acts of terrorism. Even churches aren't immune to the kind of violence that can push whole communities into a situational crisis. At one time or another almost all people will find themselves struggling to find a spiritual path in the midst of a situational crisis.

DEALING WITH CRISES

The goals of crisis management are to encourage each person to:

- grieve "successfully," which means to fully experience grief, to let go of it, and come back to life whole again
- accept the truth, even though that truth may be the necessity of medication or long-term therapy, or even living with the help of a caregiver
- accept the event and accept, and even rejoice in, that he or she has been changed by it
- learn to manage his or her life again, with all the demands made upon it

- learn what is and what isn't under his or her control (often people turn to religion or some form of spirituality for this purpose)
- experience pleasure and joy again

In these ways a person who has been hurt can be healed, and can feel again that living life is manageable and has its rewards.

GETTING YOUR CHURCH READY FOR CRISIS INTERVENTION

Most crisis periods last only six to eight weeks with or without assistance. Certainly during this period people in crisis will have many needs that they can't take care of by themselves. So, to be helpful, you must respond as early as possible.

Keep in mind that the way a person responds to a crisis is highly individualistic, and is partly determined by a person's age, gender, cultural variations, life experiences, and religious beliefs. Each person is a special case. Some people welcome generosity. Other people, who are more private, may be leery of it.

When intervention is appropriate, you need to learn all that you can about the crisis:

- Who was involved?
- What happened?
- What is the person in crisis feeling and thinking?
- How does this person usually deal with stressful events?
- To whom does he or she turn for support?

If the person expresses thoughts of killing him or herself (or others) or you believe that the situation is beyond your ability to intervene, you must help the person find a health care professional who can better assess the risk for self-harm and the need for more intense treatment.

Most communities maintain at least one crisis hot line number to provide immediate assistance during times of emotional emergency. These hotlines are usually staffed twenty-four hours a day, seven days a week by specially trained volunteers. Be sure that you have the local crisis hot line number available at all times so that when the need arises, you can make contact and initiate assistance.

SUICIDE

The act of suicide, or attempting suicide, is the ultimate statement of spiritual distress. Suicide is the ninth leading cause of death in the United States, and the third cause of death for fifteen- to twenty-four-year-olds. In fact, someone dies every seventeen minutes as a result of suicide in the United States. For every successful suicide, there are ten attempts. That means that today a good many people are in critical spiritual distress.

Some of the risk factors for self-destructive behavior include:

- recent or perceived loss (death of a loved one, unemployment, divorce)
- chronic medical illness
- age (especially fifteen to twenty-four; sixty-five and older)
- history of suicide attempts
- mental illness (mood disorders, substance abuse, schizophrenia, borderline or antisocial personality disorder)
- depressed mood
- family history of suicidal behavior
- hopelessness
- changes in appetite, sleeping patterns, and activity levels
- social withdrawal

Experts suggest that eighty percent of people who commit suicide *do* give some warning signs.

Treating the suicidal person is beyond the scope of the health ministry program. However, your congregation *should* be prepared to respond to the person at-risk for self-harm. If a person in your congregation is experiencing one of the "risk factors" listed above, or is showing some of the "warning signs," ask this person directly, "Are you planning to kill yourself?"

This question does not plant an idea in the head of a person who isn't thinking it already. Instead, asking the question gives the per-

---

THE WARNING SIGNS OF SUICIDE

Giving away prized possessions

A depression that goes on for a while

Talking about committing suicide or making suicide threats

Changes in habits

Increases in drug or alcohol use

Sudden change in behavior (such as being positive after days of being sullen).

---

son a chance to talk about suicidal thoughts. Those can be very lonely thoughts, so the chance to air them can bring great relief. *The company of a caring listener can allow a person to unlock dark thoughts, and, in that way, the person is no longer alone—and the negative thoughts may no longer have quite the power they had.*

Most suicidal people will talk about their pain when directly asked. If they confirm your suspicions, stay with the person and assist him or her in finding help through their health care provider, the state or local mental health system, or the local emergency room. Take every threat seriously!

A SECOND STAGE OF CRISIS INTERVENTION

After you have listened patiently and attentively, *encourage the person to use coping strategies that have been helpful in the past.* These may include problem-solving techniques, meditation, music, prayer, and exercise. You might even ask the person to name ten things he or she likes to do, and if they can't name five, name at least one. That one could be a basis for coping.

Get family and friends involved as a support system to the person in crisis. Mobilizing people who care about and understand the one who is suffering can make a strong difference in the recovery process. Their very presence may provide comfort.

In *practical ways*, also, this caring group helps ease the burden of the person in crisis. For example, a friend might come over to watch the children for a few hours every day so that the person in crisis can meditate. Other family and friends may simply let the person know, strongly and clearly, that when the person is ready, they are eager to help.

Remember that there are times that a person has to grieve. Only by living through our grief can we be ready to start coping.

Once the person in crisis has begun to cope, with the help of loved ones and friends, the next step is for you and the person in crisis to *review what has been* gained by meeting the crisis. At first that can be a difficult step for someone who has recently felt devastated. But people *do* often come out of crisis stronger in character, or soul, than they were before.

SOME QUESTIONS YOU CAN ASK

You can help people toward that strength by asking the right questions:

- What do they now know about life or other people or themselves that they didn't know before the crisis?
- What new coping strategies have they developed?
- How might they respond to similar situations in the future? (This type of reflection helps them to look forward to a time when their strength is greater than it has been or even is now.)

COMMUNITIES OF FAITH IN TIMES OF CRISIS

How can communities of faith respond specifically to crises of their parishioners and of the larger community? Here are some "strategies":

- Invoke the use of private and group prayer for members in crisis. This provides them a connection to God and lets them know the congregation is caring for them.

- Invite people who are experiencing a crisis to join specific prayer groups; the scriptural guidance they receive will have direct meaning for their suffering.
- A minister may wish to announce, from the pulpit or in a newsletter, that he or she, or specially trained lay leaders from the congregation, are available to provide comfort and counsel. Often the minister or the lay leaders can recommend resources both inside and outside the church that will strengthen the support network of people in crisis. Those resources will be both inside and outside the church.
- Volunteers can organize to help. For people in crisis, the simplest tasks can be overwhelming. Doing the laundry or grocery shopping or tidying up the house can feel like too much. Such ordinary tasks require energy that people in heartbreak and grief probably cannot spare. When volunteers perform such tasks, people in crisis can attend to other, deeper issues and responsibilities.

ANTICIPATING CRISES

Crises, like sicknesses, are often better averted than cured. The loss of a loved one, retirement, and aging are examples of changes all of us can anticipate. Further, people find themselves in financial or legal crises, and face other life problems that, if prepared for, need not be experienced as crises.

Your congregation can help members anticipate the potential emotional impact of, say, retirement, by running a series of programs for people who expect to retire in the next five to ten years. Members will learn the inherent stresses associated with retirement and prepare for a world without the daily routine of work. Future retirees will learn the importance of cultivating new hobbies and activities such as volunteering, perhaps at the church. They can also start thinking about the financial and social implications that their retirement status will bring. In this way, retirees get a chance to examine and discuss their feelings about retiring.

For situational crises like divorce, a *divorce support group* can be helpful. Though marriages end for a variety of reasons, divorce is usually stressful and may precipitate a crisis. You can support people going through divorce either through special scheduled programs or through an ongoing support group. The key here is to employ a non-judgmental approach that allows the participants to openly explore their feelings and thoughts while receiving emotional and spiritual encouragement. We all know that being able to talk about our hopes and fears can often strengthen our hopes and diminish our fears.

LARGE-SCALE CRISES

When large-scale catastrophes occur, such as the terrorist attacks of September 11, 2001, the federal government may deploy organized support like the National Crisis Response Teams. Your church might serve as a sanctuary for the suffering or as a base for the crisis team. Members of your health team may be able to assist these professionals in providing relief to people affected by the disaster.

Remember that a crisis period can extend long after the first few days following the event. As members of the local community, you have the ability to provide interventions long after the crisis team has left the area.

The National Organization for Victim Assistance (NOVA) has laid out guidelines for crisis intervention in the event of a disaster. *Helping the victims feel safe and secure* is the first goal of crisis intervention. Besides protecting the victims from physical harm, the intervention team must ensure that the basic needs of food, shelter, and clothes are met. They must also try to provide emotional and spiritual nurture, and that, too, can fall directly under the province of your ministry.

The second goal is to *provide victims the chance to talk about the experience, release their feelings, and validate their reactions.* People respond to crisis differently. Some show steely courage, others immediately look to the needs of their fellows, and some may be paralyzed or even hysterical with fear and dismay. Victims have to be reassured that there is no right way to respond. In crisis, each of us can only be who we are at that terrible moment. It is your job to help people who may feel that they broke down under pressure and should therefore be ashamed. Your presence and support can be powerful here. Remember that even those who held up strongly and bravely at the time of the crisis may suffer an emotional aftermath, in response to what they saw and what they did. They too need to talk about their experience, and about how, afterwards, they feel.

The third goal is to *help victims to anticipate and prepare to deal with the aftermath of the disaster*. Financial issues, legal concerns, spiritual distress, along with practical issues like funeral arrangements may be pressing considerations. At any on these levels, the congregation can offer far-reaching assistance to the victims and survivors.

REFERENCE

Bell, Geneveva E.: *My Rose: An African Amercian Mother's Story of AIDS*. Pilgrim Press, 1997.

Worden, J. William: *Grief Counseling & Grief Therapy: A Guide for the Mental Health Professional, A Handbook for the Mental Health Practitioner*. 2nd Ed. New York: Springer Publishing, 1991.

TEN

COPING WITH DEATH

Joe was the youth pastor at a small church in the Midwest. He and his wife, Lisa, had tried to have a baby for three years. When she finally became pregnant, they were ecstatic and shared the news with their family and their church friends. But as Lisa's pregnancy progressed, the doctors became concerned about the baby's development. It seemed the baby might have a rare genetic disorder that kept the brain and spinal cord from developing normally. Though Lisa carried the baby to term, their first son lived only hours after his birth.

The funeral was held at their church, and their congregation mourned with them. Lisa and Joe were heartbroken, but they also felt that God had allowed this tragedy to happen and that they must continue to trust Him. Lisa became pregnant again and lost the second child in the middle of her pregnancy. The congregation was not sure how to support the grieving couple, but when Lisa and Joe announced their wish to try again, community members found quiet ways to show them that their courage and determination were honored by their spiritual community.

Lisa's third pregnancy progressed normally, though Lisa suffered frequent panic attacks over the possibility of losing this baby, too. In the end, despite her fears, she delivered a healthy son, and the couple and their church family rejoiced.

A few years later, Joe and Lisa tried to have another child, but their fourth child was stillborn as a result of the same brain and spinal cord defects as their first baby. Now members of the congregation asked themselves why the couple continued to try to have children and "put themselves through all this grief."

Joe and Lisa entered a kind of crisis at this time. They wondered why God let them have only one healthy child but allowed the others to die. Lisa suffered from depression and Joe questioned his calling to the ministry. Coping with the deaths of these children seemed more than they could bear, and the congregation did not know how to comfort them.

Lisa and Joe's situation was terrible to endure. Yet every day, within our own churches, many people are trying to cope with death and other serious losses. Think of how many people in your church died within the past year, and then think about how many family members and friends had to cope with those losses. Quite possibly you have had to cope with the death of someone dear to you.

SUDDEN DEATH

When a death occurs suddenly and unexpectedly, the family may be left in shock and disbelief. Friends may not know what to say or how to comfort them. Lingering questions haunt the family:

- Could the accident or sickness have been prevented?
- Could I have done something to change the outcome?
- Why did this happen to us?

Consider Ellen and Mark's story. They were having marital problems and it began to look like divorce. Their oldest son, John, was a senior in high school—a nice kid, popular in his high school choir. One month before graduation, when John was driving a car, he was killed by a drunk driver. His parents and siblings were devastated.

The family did not attend church regularly and had little social support in the community except for a few close friends. Ellen told her best friend that she felt numb. She wanted the world to just stop when John died, but it kept on going. Ellen was like a robot, going through the motions but oblivious to life around her.

At John's funeral, his friends gave Ellen her greatest comfort. They wore their choir sweaters to honor him, and set up a scholarship in his name. But Mark and Ellen could not comfort each other because of their already rocky relationship, and soon after John's death, the marriage ended. John's brother and sister, living with their mom, now had to cope with both the loss of their brother and their parent's divorce. Both children rebelled against their parents' authority and moved out on their own as soon as they were able.

It took Ellen years to come to terms with her son's death, but she was finally able to use her own experience to help comfort and support other parents who had lost children. Mark was never able to deal with his loss and turned to alcohol for comfort. He died of liver cirrhosis a few years later.

Mark and Ellen coped with the death of their son in their own ways. Mark's way was to avoid his feelings. Ellen was finally able to channel her energies into her own healing and use her insight to help others.

At one level, we know that death is an inevitable consequence of being human, but we avoid talking or even thinking about death because it makes us uncomfortable. So when death strikes close to home, it always comes as a terrible surprise. If sudden death is accidental and the victim is a child, survivors may feel overwhelmed by powerlessness and even guilt. They may endlessly play the game of "what if?" Would John be alive if he'd gotten in the car a few seconds later, if I had stopped him for a hug? Should I have let him go out? Should I have let him drive? Why didn't I offer to take him? What if I had made him stay home? What if I had been driving instead? These questions can haunt the family and friends who remain alive. They can gnaw into a person's very soul.

Sudden death is relatively rare, usually the result of an accident or a heart attack or stroke. A person who has suffered a sudden death in the family may need a longer time to grieve and adjust than one who has been able to prepare ahead of time for a death and whose grieving took in the entire dying process. To bring comfort to people who have been shocked by the sudden death of a loved one, review the support strategies that you learned in Chapter 9.

DEATH FROM CHRONIC ILLNESS

Most people die from chronic illnesses. When death is near, the person and family often have some time to prepare for the end of life. Congregations can help by knowing how to support the dying person and his or her family.

Even though people might prefer to die at home, the most common place of death is in the hospital. While hospitals provide necessary medical care, hospital personnel are often neither specially trained nor equipped to promote the dignified death the person and family would like. Therefore, family members must do what they can to provide the atmosphere they need. Hospital personnel will respect their wishes, as long as what the family does is in harmony with hospital procedures.

In order to ensure that the patient can die with dignity, planning is essential. While the person is still alert, he or she should be encouraged to make these decisions:

- whether to die in the hospital or at home
- whether to allow medical treatment that will keep the patient alive past the point where there is any chance for recovery or for conscious life
- how to dispose of property
- whether to donate organs
- who will care for the surviving family
- who will pay the bills
- who will take over a business
- what form should the funeral ceremony take

And so on.

Helping a person to die at home, even when there are a number of family members ready to assist, can be very challenging. Ordering hospital beds and other equipment, administering medication and other care, dealing with crises—all these challenges and more can seem overwhelming if no experienced person is at hand.

HOSPICE CARE

Blessedly, there is a service called Hospice. Hospice is a unique program that promotes a peaceful and dignified death for people with terminal illness. Nurses specially trained in end-of-life care will teach family members what to expect and work with them to keep the dying person comfortable, while meeting the dying person's health care needs.

Hospice nurses provide care for the dying person and the family from the time they enter the program until after the person's death. This is holistic care in which the person's physical, emotional, spiritual, and psychosocial needs are addressed. The family plays an important role and is encouraged to be part of the Hospice team of professionals who will care for the dying person.

Pain management is a major concern of the patient and family, and Hospice nurses and physicians are especially trained to help control pain through the use of appropriate medications and other techniques that can ease the stresses on the dying body:

Hospice programs operate in a variety of settings. They may:

- have their own facility
- be part of a long-term care facility such as a nursing home
- provide services within the acute-care hospital
- be run by the local visiting nurse's association

Churches with congregational health programs can work with hospice professionals to help in caring for the dying person. Hospice workers know how to teach others how to provide comfort during the dying process. The hospice programs can give dying people quality care and allow them to have peaceful deaths at home surrounded by family and friends, if that is their wish.

You can find the nearest Hospice through your hospital or local library, or you can call Hospice directly at (800) 658–8898, or (703) 243–5900.

THE DYING PROCESS

Much of our fear about being present at the death of another person comes because we don't know what to expect. People who truly want to help dying friends or family members hold themselves back because they don't know how to be helpful. This chapter makes suggestions that can help you help people in your congregation or community.

First, before you can be helpful, you must understand the process. The final days and hours before a person dies are precious to him or her and the family. Ideally, the practical questions have been settled by now. This time is for farewells and deep communication; a time when love shows itself in the presence of death.

How a person wants to die is an individual choice. Some people might want music playing, or to have a prayer or other text read to them. Others want silence. By being sensitive and supporting the wishes of the dying person, you help him or her leave this earthly life in a peaceful, settled way. To help ensure that peace, the person should feel free, without outside emotional pressure, to name the loved ones he or she wants near.

SIGNS OF DEATH

No one can accurately predict exactly when death will occur, but certain physical signs tell us death is near. As family members keep vigil with the dying loved one, it may become more and more difficult to watch the physical changes that occur as death approaches. But by knowing what will happen and discussing these changes openly, everyone becomes more comfortable with the process of dying. A Hospice nurse or your congregational health nurse can educate you on what to expect at each stage of dying.

Some dying people seem to sense when death will come. Some wait for a special event (such as a birthday, a wedding in the family, a special anniversary) before dying, as if, only when they have tied up loose ends, can they let go of life.

Physical Signs of Dying

Dying involves slowing the processes of the entire body. The signs and symptoms listed below can begin months or minutes before death. Each dying person will die in his or her own way. Some people exhibit many of the following signs, and others far fewer:

- Weakness, fatigue, more time spent sleeping
- Being less responsive to surroundings
- Confusion, restlessness, disorientation
- Decreased eating and drinking (may not have a good swallow reflex)
- Fever
- Brief bursts of energy
- Loss of bowel and bladder function

Universal symptoms that a person will die soon include:

- decreased urine output until no urine is being produced
- arms and legs become cold and mottled
- heart rate and blood pressure change significantly
- breathing patterns change and there may be a moist sound and short, gasping breaths

Once these signs and symptoms appear, it is wise to inform family members who wish to be present at the time of death. However, understand that even when a person has stopped eating and drinking and is receiving no nutrition or intravenous fluids, it can still take days or weeks for death to occur.

This time is terribly difficult for family members as they keep watch, knowing death is near. Sometimes people feel guilt and anguish. They may fear their loved one is suffering.

Let them know that prolonging life through artificial means when death is imminent does not change the outcome significantly. If end-of-life care has been planned to occur naturally and with sufficient pain medication (if needed), a dying person usually *doesn't* suffer. Once again, if the family gets help from Hospice nurses and other experts, and can foresee the stages of dying, the loved one can die in reasonable peace.

SIGNS AND SYMPTOMS OF DEATH

When death comes, you will see the following:

- No heart beat, breathing, or blood pressure
- No response to pain or verbal stimuli
- Pale, cold skin
- Pupils are fixed and the eyes may remain open
- Stool and/or urine may be expelled
- The mouth may be open as the jaw relaxes

Death generally must be confirmed by a physician, nurse, or coroner. Know the laws in your state, or ask your Hospice nurse for information. If you are alone in the room at the time of death:

- write down the time
- have phone numbers of people to call when death occurs
- if the person has donated the body to science (such as a medical school), know what number to call to notify them
- observe the person's wishes as to cultural and religious rites and practices regarding treatment of the body

EMOTIONAL TASKS IN THE DYING PROCESS

Dying people can experience a range of feelings, including negative ones like anger, denial, and grief. They may also experience fear— fear of dying alone or of being abandoned, fear of the unknown, fear that they've left too much unfinished business, including emotional or spiritual business.

Dying people often need to repair relationships broken in the past and simply set their relational house in order. As death becomes inevitable, they may show a heightened interest in spiritual issues. In some cases, the person may wish for frequent talks with his pastor or spiritual leader. Even people who have had little interest in spiritual things before may now express great spiritual need.

Dying people often review their lives, searching for meaning and purpose. They may reminisce about their accomplishments, joys, and sorrows. They may wish to look at photographs. They may want to spend some of their last energy settling financial affairs or even planning their own funerals. Some dying people wish to buy presents for relatives, to be given to them on special occasions after their death. Others make video tapes or write letters to loved ones to be read after they pass away. Each of these acts is an expression of the last wishes of the dying person.

Congregational members can support the dying person by helping to write or mail letters, by making trips to the store to purchase special items, or helping make phone calls. The importance of these activities as aids to a peaceful death should never be underestimated.

OTHER WAYS TO HELP THE DYING PERSON

If the dying person is your friend or loved one, there can be special issues between you. For example, does he or she wish you to be part of this process? Allow the person the right to make the choice freely, and if, for whatever reason, he or she doesn't ask for your company, accept that decision.

If the person does want you to be involved, learn as much as you can about his or her condition. If the person is receiving Hospice services, the Hospice nurse will be able to teach you about appropriate care, and—if the dying person has given permission—will share information with you about his or her condition.

Learn what the person and family wish your role to be in the dying process. Whatever your job is, you need to do it with a generous heart in order to comfort the dying person. This is a job that requires patience and sympathy. Don't take it on unless you are sure you can complete it.

You can be of help to the dying person by:

- keeping a cool washcloth on the person's forehead
- just sitting and holding hands
- reading scripture or praying
- making phone calls, to the pastor or other family members, to keep them informed as death approaches
- being an advocate for the dying person

- helping support the person's wishes
- intervening if necessary to help others understand what the dying person wants
- helping to arrange for the person to die in the place of his or her choice (it is usually unwise to transfer the dying person to another place right before death, because it can be upsetting to the person and family at a time when peace should be promoted)
- knowing beforehand the signs of impending death and the care the person might need as this time approaches.
- communicating openly and honestly (dying people often have a heightened awareness of whether people are speaking to them with candor; the fact that the dying person is inviting you to participate in the end of his or her life assumes truth and trust between you)
- answering honestly if the person asks for information about his or her condition, but be sure your information is correct
- asking a family member or health care provider to help with things you are uncomfortable discussing
- just being there: Your presence is the most comforting gift you can give to your dying loved one.
- surrounding the person with whatever he or she loves most, such as rosary beads or the Bible, a stuffed animal, family pictures or other personal belongings collected through the years. Perhaps just having the grandchildren visit is enough. Whatever it is, do your best to accommodate.
- supporting the person at the end of the spiritual journey by helping with activities that bring spiritual comfort, whether prayer, Bible reading, listening to sacred music, or just discussing anticipation or fears of the life hereafter.

PROVIDING SUPPORT AND COMFORT TO THE FAMILY

Once a person has died, do not forget the needs of the family and friends who are left to grieve. They may have a need to talk about that person's life and death. They may wish to look at pictures and the person's personal belongings. Laugh with them and cry with them. Hug them and sit with them. Let them talk and tell stories even if they tell the same ones over and over.

When people have had the chance to prepare for death, many of their personal matters may be settled, but don't assume that they are. Ask the family if there is anything you can do to help to settle unfinished business. Offer specific help such as meal preparation or transportation.

Sometimes, once the person is buried and the helper is drawn back into his or her own life, grieving is forgotten. As time passes, think about what you can do to show the mourners that you share in their continued sorrow.

Consider Sarah, who lost a baby through miscarriage early in her pregnancy. Sarah felt a terrible sense of loss. The baby was conceived out of wedlock, but Sarah loved the unborn baby deeply and had intended to raise it herself. Now the baby was dead, and Sarah felt deserted by her family and scorned by the church, for what they considered her sin.

Nan was an older woman from the church who had known Sarah since she was a child. Now Nan, seeing that Sarah had been left alone, stepped in to care for her. She visited Sarah daily just after the baby died, and kept close contact afterwards. She was genuinely able to share Sarah's sorrow, and make Sarah feel less abandoned. Nan's concern didn't stop there. Each year, she sent Sarah a rose on the morning of the date of the miscarriage to let her know that she remembered her loss. Nan's acts of kindness and Christian care spoke deeply to Sarah. It helped her to return to her life and even to keep her faith. Eventually she became an active member of the congregation—but in another church.

There are many ways a congregation can show its continuing concern. Joyce's oldest child, Betsy, was diagnosed with breast cancer in her thirties and died five years later, leaving behind a husband and three children.

The death hit Joyce very hard. She had three other children, but, unlike Betsy, they had moved out of town. Joyce was a widow and felt quite isolated. Her friends attended the funeral together, but their support didn't stop there. When Joyce was ready, they began to take her out to the movies and join her for dinner. They kept her involved in church activities and used her talents to help plan special events in the children's ministries. They even organized fundraising walks during National Cancer Month that they dedicated to Betsy's memory. In all these ways they helped Joyce to heal.

Sudden death can leave a parent especially devastated. When Mark's only son, Scott, was killed in a hunting accident, Mark, a single father, was so overwhelmed with grief that he couldn't bear to go through Mark's things, and left his bedroom exactly as it had been at the time of his death.

Mark mentioned his sense of helplessness to the men in his Bible study group, and a group of his friends offered to help him go through Mark's things. For Mark, the task now became liberating. Sorting Scott's things with his friends, Mark was able to reminisce about the joy his son's life had brought him. This process brought healing and some sense of closure to Mark.

A PEACEFUL DEATH

Advances in pain management and palliative care (professional medical and nursing care that is not aimed at curing but at providing comfort)has enabled people who might otherwise have died painful and tormented deaths to die peacefully and comfortably.

Congregational members can help create a peaceful death for a loved one by providing the right words of spiritual comfort, but in order to help another person die peacefully, you must first know peace yourself. Before you step into the role of companion to a person who is dying, examine your own feelings about death, perhaps through conversation with a friend or someone in the health ministry especially able to explore these feelings.

Expect to have fears and feelings of discomfort that can work against the comfort you are trying to bring. People who want to help learn that they can work through the fears and awkwardness that an encounter with death may often bring. Love and simple good intention are all that is required. In these situations, as in so many others, love does find a way.

For all our discomfort and fear in the face of death, people who believe in a better life than the one here on earth can also find that death brings release and freedom. They may look forward to release from pain and sorrow. As the apostle Paul stated in 2 Corinthians 5:8, "... to be absent from the body and to be present with the Lord" is the hope of all Christians.

In the account of the crucifixion in the gospel of Mark, Jesus tells the repentant thief, "today you will be with me in Paradise." This passage is a significant source of encouragement for all Christians. Other religions also hold out the promise of release.

For Christians, death marks the end of the troubled earthly life and the immediate beginning of heavenly reward. Some people may look upon death as the desired end of life that leads to a much better place—in spiritual company, at last, with the object of their faith. These beliefs help many people have a peaceful death as they finish their earthly race.

ELEVEN

ETHICAL AND LEGAL CONSIDERATIONS

There are ethical and legal dilemmas associated with the end of life, and when people encounter them for the first time, in a time of grief, they can be hard to bear. Here is an example for your congregational health group to discuss.

Edith was an eighty-six year old widowed Anglo-American woman with a history of heart disease and stroke. Edith had had heart surgery and there had been complications that brought her back to the hospital a few times for stays of several weeks.

Only a year after her surgery, Edith suffered a massive stroke that left her unable to speak or eat on her own. She could not move one side of her body. Edith had no control over bowel and bladder function. She was also now blind.

What the family physician told Edith's family was the hardest kind of news. Given Edith's condition, he said, it was virtually impossible that Edith would ever again enjoy what most of us consider a dignified life. To be sure, she might be kept alive for a while longer if they kept her on IVs and tube feedings. But Edith could only be kept alive in a vegetative state. Unable to interact, understand, or move by herself, she would need continuous care. In medical terms, she would experience no "quality of life."

A few years before she died, Edith had anticipated such a

moment by making a "Living Will," stating she did not wish her life to be prolonged by artificial means if her death was imminent.

After their talk with the doctor, the family sat down in the hospital's family room to talk among themselves. In the end, they felt they must be guided by Edith's will. That meant stopping the intravenous fluids and tube feedings that were keeping her alive, and continuing only her IV pain medication as needed.

Then the family waited for Edith to die. For the first day they kept vigil at Edith's hospital bedside, but one of Edith's daughters, who had been her primary caregiver, wanted to take her home to die.

At the daughter's home, family members cared for Edith for several days, but they became more and more distraught as the days went on. They hadn't contacted Hospice, and were finding the task of seeing Edith through her dying more than they were ready for.

The day after she returned to the hospital, five days after removal of the fluids and nutrition, Edith seemed to rally. She opened her eyes more often and moved her unaffected arm. The family now felt that they might have made the wrong decision, but Edith's doctor told them that his diagnosis remained the same: Edith had suffered extensive brain damage from the stroke and would not regain any quality of life.

The family was in real anguish. Several of them were sure that Edith could hear when they spoke to her and sometimes responded. One of her daughters felt that they were "starving their mother to death." But in the end, the family decided that they were doing what Edith would have wanted. She was the one who always said that as long as she had her yard to walk around in she had enough. They couldn't imagine Edith wanting to live in her present state.

Edith lingered for several days more without fluids and nutrition. She was given pain medications whenever it seemed she was uncomfortable. The nursing staff turned her regularly and provided skin care. She gradually showed swelling in her lower extremities and her urine output decreased. She slept more and more.

On the ninth day, Edith passed away quietly and peacefully. But several members of the family, specially the daughters who were closest to Edith, continued to feel guilty. They felt that, whatever the doctor said, Edith's movements had been potential signs of recovery. And now Edith was gone.

It took the daughters a long time, and some counseling, to get past their feelings of guilt.

DISCUSSING EDITH'S CASE

What we consider morally or spiritually correct is a matter of individual convictions and beliefs. Especially when it comes to the hard questions that can surround dying, there are no simple answers. That's why it is wise to think about these situations ahead of time. Thinking through the questions in advance can often teach you how you want to respond when the actual situation arises.

Once you have had the chance to think Edith's case through, discuss your considered views with others in the group. Such discussions aren't likely to produce a perfect consensus, but afterwards the participants will be better able to make tough decisions when they need to.

Here are questions that might guide your discussion:

- What do you think about withdrawing treatment from a person who has been certified as terminally ill and without "quality of life"?
- What are the conflicting points of view in this situation?
- Based on the facts given, would you have made the same decision Edith's family did, or a different one? Why?
- What is the difference between withholding and withdrawing treatment? Does one seem more ethically or morally acceptable than the other? Why or why not?
- What ethical and spiritual principles were followed by the family in this case?
- What if the family's wishes and Edith's wishes were in conflict?
- Is there anything about this scenario that makes you uncomfortable?
- If you were a member of Edith's church family, what could you have done to comfort her or the family during this time?
- What is the pastor's responsibility in this situation?

- What might you say to the daughters who are experiencing guilt over their decision?
- What special scriptures could comfort this family?

Edith's story presents a common dilemma that families face— whether to withhold or withdraw medical treatment from a loved one.

UNDERSTANDING ADVANCE DIRECTIVES

Advance directives are legal documents in which a competent person states his or her wishes in advance for the medical care he or she wants in the event of a terminal illness. In other words, a person states whether he or she wishes to be kept alive or be allowed to die naturally when there is no hope of recovery as certified by a physician.

There are several types of advance directives. These include:

- a living will
- power of attorney
- a life-prolonging procedures document
- appointment of a health care representative

All adults have the right to issue these documents to express their wishes. Preparing them allows others to know what your wishes are and allows them to make decisions on your behalf if you are not able to do so. But as you learned from Edith's story, no document can take the place of open and honest communication between family members.

DECLARATION OF LIVING WILL

A "Living Will" is a legal document drawn up when a person who is "mentally competent and of sound mind" determines that he or she wishes to die a natural death. Two conditions must be met for the "Living Will" to be in effect:

- The person must be terminally ill, with death being imminent, without the help of artificial life support.
- An attending physician must certify that the person is in this condition.

"Living Wills" are null and void for a woman who is pregnant, since in such cases the physician must also try to protect the life of the unborn child.

In your "Living Will," you can stipulate whether or not you wish to have artificially supplied nutrition and hydration to prevent your death, or you can leave this decision to family members to make if the situation should arise.

APPOINTMENT OF A HEALTH CARE REPRESENTATIVE

This legal document allows one person to appoint another to make decisions on his or her behalf regarding health and medical treatment. If the dying person can still communicate, the health care representative can discuss these decisions with him or her. But if the person is unable to communicate, the health care representative can make decisions alone.

There is usually a stipulation in this document that pain medications should be provided, even if they would unintentionally hasten death, in order to provide a comfortable and peaceful death.

POWER OF ATTORNEY

A power of attorney document allows one person to act on another person's behalf for decisions regarding personal property, real estate, banking, and numerous other records or documents. The person granted power of attorney can sign legal documents such as the other person's payroll checks or estate transactions.

Such powers of attorney can be granted between husbands and wives or others, while they are in a healthy state, to allow each other free access to all business transactions. Or, the power of attorney can be in effect only upon certification by a physician that the person is unable to manage his own financial affairs effectively.

LIFE-PROLONGING PROCEDURES DECLARATION

In contrast to the "Living Will," the life-prolonging procedures document allows a person to specify that everything should be done to sustain his life even in the event of inevitable death. The person can specify in advance which treatments he wishes to have. These can be very specific. For example, a person may wish to have nutrition and hydration, but refuse to be put on a ventilator. They may specify having IVs but refuse CPR.

ETHICAL AND SPIRITUAL PRINCIPLES

People of faith, like all people, sometime run into moral dilemmas in which there seem to be no good alternatives. To help in such cases, ethicists recognize several foundational ethical principles. We present them here in the light of Christian faith, although these principles are also shared by other faiths.

Autonomy is the right of a person to make his or her own decisions. We have a duty to respect the personal liberty and values of other people, even when we disagree with their religious beliefs. In this way, we uphold both their personal spirituality and our own.

Beneficence means "to actively do good." Christians who follow the golden rule by doing unto others as they would have them do unto them are practicing beneficence. (Of course, this principle assumes that people wish to have good done to them). This ethical principle also means that we try to prevent harm from coming to others. Scriptures support the quest for doing good, even to our enemies (Matthew 5:44).

Non-maleficence is similar to beneficence, but means "to do no harm." This rule says that we should not treat people badly or try to hurt them. It is less proactive than the principle of beneficence. In the Sermon on the Mount, Jesus' taught that if a person hurts you, you should turn the other cheek (Matthew 5:39–42). Romans 12:17–21 adds that we are not to return evil for evil, but to treat even our enemies with kindness, and to overcome evil with good.

Formal or distributive justice refers to treating people equally, but usually within the limits of available resources, and according to their needs. In the early church, during the time after Christ's death, everybody shared their belongings with each other, so that every person was cared for according to their needs (Acts 2: 44–46). This practice, combined with their daily worship, resulted in "gladness and singleness of heart" and growth of the Church (Acts 2:46–47).

Veracity is the duty to tell the truth and *fidelity* refers to the principle of honoring one's commitments and remaining loyal. These principles are also supported in the Bible. Ephesians 4:15 talks about "speaking the truth in love." Proverbs tells how God hates the lying tongue, people who tell lies about their neighbors, and people who sow discord (Proverbs 6:16–19). Faithfulness being rewarded has numerous references in Scripture, and we are encouraged to remain steadfast (Matthew 24:45; Hebrews 11; Ecclesiastes 9:9; 1 Corinthians 15:58; Colossians 3: 23–24; Galatians 5:1; 2 Timothy 4: 7–8).

Privacy refers to the rule of respecting people's rights to limit access to certain things about themselves and is closely related to *confidentiality*, a term often used in health care, which means that professionals have a duty not to reveal information about a person that was shared in a trusted relationship (such as nurse-patient confidentiality). Again, the Scriptures encourage men to live peaceably and to keep their own households. We are instructed not to be gossips, but to respect the privacy of others. Proverbs 11:13 states, "a talebearer revealeth secrets, but he that is of a faithful spirit concealeth the matter."

Legal considerations are also a part of what we think of as foundational ethics.

All people have an obligation to live within the laws of their places of residence, even in cases where personal moral judgment might conflict with the law. Though people of faith may answer to a higher authority, they are still accountable to act as responsible citizens and to respect the laws of the earthly powers.

In 1 Timothy 2:1–2, Christians are encouraged to pray and offer intercessions "for kings, and for all that are in authority, that we may lead a quiet and peaceable life in all godliness and honesty." In Romans 13: 1–7, Paul writes that we are to be subject to the governmental powers, and that they are allowed to be in power because of God's ultimate authority.

This idea means that even people of faith, who claim to answer to God as the ultimate authority, must abide by the laws of earthly government. Dilemmas arise when the rules of the earthly government are in conflict with the rules that govern our faith. Further discussion of these dilemmas is beyond the scope of this book.

Churches that wish to start a congregational health program should be guided by both ethical and spiritual principles. These foundational principles do not conflict with each other. If you steer by their light, your church will succeed in its efforts to promote good health and provide help to people who are ill, dying, or bereaved.

SOME FINAL NUTS AND BOLTS

Starting a health ministry is a spiritual opportunity but it is also a practical responsibility. We will end with a few practical reminders.

How to Ensure Competent Staffing

Be sure that the people working on your programs are well trained. Trained staff should include the parish nurse, volunteers for any of the various tasks we've outlined, program speakers, and discussion leaders. (See Chapter Five for further discussion.)

In the case of speakers or other outside experts, check references, get referrals, and be sure the person's educational level is appropriate to the task. You have a legal and moral obligation to be sure that the information you provide is the best available.

Professionals hired to act as coordinators or parish nurses should maintain current licensure and continue with their education. Keep records of their credentials. A planning committee should discuss all policies with professional staff, and policies, when established, should be written down.

Go and Serve

Remember it is not the job of a congregational health program to provide medical care for everyone. *The main goal is to educate.* That mission frees the church from legal entanglements that could arise if the church actually practiced medicine.

The smart way to avoid potential legal problems is to use wise judgment in developing programs, and to make sure that the people involved in planning and teaching are well qualified. Open and honest communication and a program based upon ethical and spiritual principles are still other assurances against legal problems.

Keep in mind that your purpose is not to replace, or act as a substitute for, medical services or facilities, but to help promote the health of the members of your congregation and community through education. Your program forms a link to the health care system for people who may not have had one. Such programs can help put people in touch with much needed resources and help spread information that will result in better health for all.

In Matthew (5: 3–4), Jesus speaks to the people, saying, "Blessed are the poor in spirit, for theirs is the kingdom of heaven. Blessed are those who mourn, for they will be comforted." Every culture has developed forms for coping with the universal experiences of crisis and grief. In these forms, crises are recognized and celebrated as part of the whole of the human experience. The faith community is especially gifted for serving people who suffer. Go and serve!

INDEX